TURN THE PAGE

For Every Soul That's Been Broken
but Is Still Beloved

JORDYN ST.JOHN

To my family, for your steady love and support through every season.

To my husband, whose gentle strength, unwavering faith, and love made me believe in love again. You loved my broken parts and healed my heart in ways I never expected.

And to Jesus, my first love, my healer, and my constant. You never abandoned me or let me go. You've turned every scar into a testimony of grace. This is Your story, and I pray it brings You honor and glory with every word.

CONTENTS

INTRODUCTION

There was a time when I didn't recognize myself, when the girl in the mirror seemed like a stranger, weighed down by guilt, confusion, and a grief I couldn't name. Abuse has a way of rewriting your story without permission. It can sneak in quietly, rearranging your sense of self, twisting the truth until you forget who you were before the damage. For a long time, I lived in that rewritten version of my story. I believed I was too broken, too far gone, and too full of shame to ever find my way back to the light. But now, after a long and honest journey of healing and growth, I can say this with clarity and confidence: I've turned the page and reclaimed my identity in Christ.

That doesn't mean the pain has vanished. I still have moments where old lies creep in, where anxiety returns without warning, and where insecurity knocks at the door. Healing doesn't mean forgetting. It means facing each wave with a stronger anchor. Now, I meet those moments not with despair, but with the deep assurance that I am not who I was. I am not what happened to me. I am not the version of myself that I became while I was in survival mode. I am a new creation, rooted in grace, held together by the One who never let me go, even when I struggled to hold on to Him.

This book was written for the woman who's lived through something she never thought she'd survive. For the one who can't stop asking, "How did I get here?" For the girl who stayed too long, who ignored the red flags, and who once mistook control for love and silence for peace. For the woman who feels she has nowhere left to turn but to the Lord. For the one searching for a Savior and desperate for some measure of peace. Whether you've walked with Him for years or are just beginning to discover Him in these pages, my prayer is that you will come to know Him as I have: the God who sees, hears, and knows the deepest parts of your pain, and who is at work in every fiber of it.

This is for every soul that's been broken but is still beloved. My prayer is that as you read, you'll begin to see your story through a new lens. Not one of shame, but one of strength. Not one of defeat, but one of deliverance. I want to help you name what happened. I want to help you understand it, grieve it, and let go of what was never yours to hold alone. But more than that, I want to show you that God is still writing your story, and the next chapter doesn't have to look like the last. Through these pages, you'll learn how to recognize abuse for what it is, how to reframe the lies you've believed, how to identify and open up to healthy relationships, and how to rebuild a life fixed not in fear, but in truth. Most of all, you'll be reminded of your identity. Not the one shaped by trauma, but the one secured by Jesus.

It's hard to connect with this kind of message without knowing the journey behind it. So let me share mine, not because my story is the focus, but because I hope it helps you make sense of yours.

I was raised in a Christian family and gave my life to Christ as a child. I showed up to church every Sunday and tried my best to please everyone. But no amount of religion prepared me for what came next. In middle school, I was groomed by someone my family trusted. That violation left me confused, ashamed, and carrying unspoken fear. That early trauma warped the way I saw love, safety, and myself.

By high school, my sense of self-worth was already fragile, and I entered into a relationship that would nearly destroy me. Over the course of two years, I endured emotional manipulation, narcissistic abuse, and physical trauma. My abuser isolated me from the people who loved me most, stripped me of my identity, and made me feel like I couldn't survive without him. And the worst part? I believed it. I stayed, not because I wanted the pain, but because I couldn't tell where love ended and fear began. I felt trapped, hopeless, and deeply ashamed.

By God's mercy, I eventually found a way out. But leaving wasn't the end; it was the beginning of a whole new battle. PTSD, memory loss, panic attacks, and nightmares followed me like shadows. I was terrified to share my story, afraid of what people would think. But through it all, my family and friends loved me with a grace that pointed me straight back to Jesus. Their forgiveness reminded me of the Savior who took on what He didn't deserve so I could be free in Him. I was reminded of the foundation that was laid for me as a child. I was being called back to the Lord in an extraordinary way. He was reminding me of a love that was gracious, slow to anger, patient, forgiving, kind, and all-knowing. Slowly and gently, God began to restore the pieces of me I thought were gone forever.

And that's where this story begins … not at the breaking, but at the rebuilding. Not at the wound, but at the healing. Because the truth is, what was meant to destroy me only drove me deeper into the arms of God. Jesus didn't just save me from the abuse; He met me in the aftermath. He didn't just call me out of the darkness; He walked with me through it. And now, God is using what I once thought was the end of my story to bring hope and new life to others.

Today, I'm walking in purpose as a worship leader, songwriter, author, survivor, and most of all, a daughter of the King. And I'm writing this book for women like you, because you're not just surviving anymore. You're here because you want to heal. You want to grow. You want to turn the page.

Throughout this book, you'll find a special section at the end of each chapter called "Your Page to Write: Where Healing Meets Action", along with some space to journal at the end of this book. These sections are designed to help you take a step—big or small —toward your own healing journey. Because the words on these pages only matter if they are lived out. Healing is not passive; it's a choice we make again and again. My challenge to you is to put truth into practice and take ownership of the story God is writing in you.

So as we begin this journey together, I want you to know that healing is hard. It will stretch you. It will stir things up. It may break your heart all over again before it begins to mend it. But it will be worth it. So take a deep breath, open your heart, be honest, be brave, and above all, trust. Trust that the God who sees you in this wilderness will walk with you into a new chapter of healing. He's not done writing your story. In fact, He's just getting started.

It's time to turn the page. Not just on your pain, but toward your purpose.

PSALM 91

Before we move forward, I want to share a passage of Scripture that became a lifeline for me in my darkest hours. Let it speak over you like it did over me, serving as a reminder that God's Word still silences fear and speaks freedom over every wounded heart (from the New International Version® Bible).

[1] Whoever dwells in the shelter of the Most High
   will rest in the shadow of the Almighty.
[2] I will say of the Lord, "He is my refuge and my fortress,
   my God, in whom I trust."
[3] Surely he will save you
   from the fowler's snare
   and from the deadly pestilence.
[4] He will cover you with his feathers,
   and under his wings you will find refuge;
   his faithfulness will be your shield and rampart.
[5] You will not fear the terror of night,
   nor the arrow that flies by day,
[6] nor the pestilence that stalks in the darkness,
   nor the plague that destroys at midday.
[7] A thousand may fall at your side,
   ten thousand at your right hand,
   but it will not come near you.
[8] You will only observe with your eyes
   and see the punishment of the wicked.

⁹ If you say, "The Lord is my refuge,"

 and you make the Most High your dwelling,

¹⁰ no harm will overtake you,

 no disaster will come near your tent.

¹¹ For he will command his angels concerning you

 to guard you in all your ways;

¹² they will lift you up in their hands,

 so that you will not strike your foot against a stone.

¹³ You will tread on the lion and the cobra;

 you will trample the great lion and the serpent.

¹⁴ "Because he loves me," says the Lord, "I will rescue him;

 I will protect him, for he acknowledges my name.

¹⁵ He will call on me, and I will answer him;

 I will be with him in trouble,

 I will deliver him and honor him.

¹⁶ With long life I will satisfy him

 and show him my salvation."

PART ONE

The Pages That Hold Hurt

IT WASN'T YOUR FAULT

"All too often, women believe it is a sign of commitment, an expression of love, to endure unkindness or cruelty, to forgive and forget. In actuality, when we love rightly, we know that the healthy, loving response to cruelty and abuse is putting ourselves out of harm's way." [1] —Bell Hooks

Guilt. Shame. Defeat.

If you're anything like me, those were the emotions that took over when the relationship finally ended. Guilt gripped my chest like a vice. I couldn't stop replaying everything in my mind over and over again. *How did I end up here? Why didn't I see the signs? How could I have been so naïve?* I blamed myself for not leaving sooner, for not recognizing the danger, for trusting someone who only knew how to take.

But somewhere in the mess of my spiraling thoughts, I remembered something my dad used to say to me as a kid: "How people treat you says more about them than it does about you." I didn't believe it at the time. Honestly, I felt like I was the problem. But here's what I've come to know deeply and fully: Abuse is never the victim's fault. Not then. Not now. Not ever.

We hear stories of abuse and instinctively think, *That would never happen to me. I'd know better.* But abuse rarely walks in wearing a warning label. It doesn't barge through the door. It slips in quietly, disguised as love, cloaked in concern. At first, it feels like safety, like attention, like passion. And by the time you see it for what it truly is, you're already entangled in it.

Danger often hides in beauty. I learned that long before I

11

could name it, standing at the edge of the Grand Canyon. My family had taken a trip there to view its breathtaking beauty. My parents warned us kids to stay far from the edge, reminding us that even something so stunning can hide deadly danger. Just one wrong step, one moment of distraction, and the fall would be swift and unforgiving.

After a day spent soaking in the vast beauty around us, we gathered that night around the TV to watch the news. There was a report about a man who had fallen to his death after placing a chair too close to the cliff's edge earlier that day. The commentators didn't hold back. "How could he be so reckless? Didn't he know better?" Their harsh words echoed in the room, and they cut deeper than anyone expected.

It's strange how, even in the face of tragedy, our first instinct as a society is to assign blame. This reaction reminds me of the way survivors of abuse are so often treated: with suspicion, judgment, and shame. "Why didn't she just leave? How could she let that happen? Didn't she know better?" But that kind of hindsight only makes sense when you're outside the pain, detached from the heartache.

That man didn't sit near the cliff because he wanted to die. Most likely, he didn't realize the danger he was in. And that's the same for so many women trapped in unhealthy relationships. When your heart is invested, your vision blurs and your judgment clouds. This is why it's so important to learn to recognize the warning signs rather than carry the burden of guilt.

The truth is this: You didn't fall because you were careless or weak. You fell because someone made you believe the ground beneath you was solid, only to pull it away without warning. You fell because someone betrayed your trust and called it love.

What is Abuse?

As defined by Legal Information Institute, abuse is "an action that intentionally harms or injures another person."[2] It can be physical, sexual, psychological, emotional, verbal, financial, digital, and spiritual. While there are many different variations, they all include intentional harm and disregarding one's boundaries. The definition of this term is one thing, but there is a deeper meaning and intention behind abuse. What abuse really means is *control*. Abuse isn't just about an isolated action; it's a pattern. It's a consistent behavior designed to manipulate, dominate, or silence someone else.

To help you better understand abuse and the warning signs, I am going to break down the various kinds in the following sections. If you can recognize the warning signs as they are happening, rather than after the fact, you can begin on your path to reclaiming your safety and your voice.

Physical Abuse

Physical abuse is often the most visible form of abuse, but it's also one of the most misunderstood. Physical abuse includes any action that causes physical harm or fear, and it often escalates over time. It's not always loud or obvious. Sometimes, it begins with control disguised as concern.

This may look like:

- Preventing someone from eating or sleeping
- Driving recklessly with someone in the car or abandoning them in unsafe places
- Trapping someone in their home or preventing them from leaving
- Forcing someone to use drugs or alcohol
- Hitting, shoving, choking, or restraining someone
- Throwing objects at someone
- Blocking access to medical help
- Threatening someone with weapons
- Stalking or following someone without consent

Sexual Abuse

Sexual abuse is one of the most painful and confusing forms of abuse because it invades the deepest parts of one's being. It's not always about violence or force. Sometimes it's subtle, wrapped in manipulation, silence, or shame. Sexual abuse includes any unwanted sexual contact or behavior, and it often leaves wounds that aren't visible but run deep. Like other forms of abuse, it can start slowly, disguised as affection or attention, making it hard to recognize, until it's already done damage.

This may look like:

- Any sexual contact or exposure involving a minor
- Any unwanted sexual touching, activity, or penetration without consent
- Grooming by manipulating trust and crossing boundaries to prepare someone for abuse
- Sexual contact involving a family member or relative

- Using someone sexually for personal gain, including sharing images without consent
- Unwanted sexual comments, advances, or gestures
- Forcing someone to film or watch pornography
- Involving others in sexual activity without someone's consent

Emotional, Psychological & Verbal Abuse

This kind of abuse doesn't leave bruises, but it cuts just as deep, sometimes deeper. It often begins subtly, cloaked in affection or care. But over time, it erodes one's identity. The goal is to gain control through shame, fear, and emotional instability. It causes someone to start to question their memory, their worth, and their very sanity.

This may look like:
- Blaming someone for another's behavior
- Accusing someone of cheating or being unfaithful
- Gaslighting by making someone question their memory or reality
- Telling someone no one else would ever want them
- Constant criticism or demeaning language
- Public humiliation or private insults
- Giving someone the silent treatment as punishment
- Making someone "pay" for mistakes
- Making someone feel worthless, broken, or crazy
- Making jokes at someone's expense
- Dismissing someone's pain as being "overly sensitive"
- Demanding credit for not physically abusing someone

Financial Abuse

Financial abuse may not sound as frightening as other forms, but it can be just as paralyzing. When someone controls one's access to money or resources, they also control their freedom. Victims of financial abuse often feel they can't leave because they won't survive on their own.

This may look like:
- Living in someone's home without contributing
- Withholding access to transportation, housing, or employment
- Hiding or denying someone access to bank accounts
- Putting someone's income into an account they can't access
- Stealing money or withholding funds as punishment
- Using someone's credit or savings without permission
- Borrowing money with no intention of paying it back
- Forcing changes to someone's will or property
- Blocking someone from getting or keeping a job

Digital Abuse

Technology can be a powerful tool or a weapon, especially in today's world. Digital abuse happens when someone uses phones, digital devices, apps, or social media to control, shame, stalk, or intimidate. It can happen out in the open or behind a screen, but the damage is just as real.

This may look like:
- Demanding someone's passwords
- Creating fake profiles online to harm one's reputation or overall well-being
- Using smart devices to monitor or track someone's location

- Sending unwanted or coercive sexual content
- Pressuring someone to send explicit images or videos
- Posting embarrassing photos online without consent
- Using AI or online communication to pretend to be someone else
- Flooding someone's phone with texts or calls to keep tabs on them
- Reading someone's messages or checking their phone without permission
- Threatening to share private information or images

Spiritual Abuse

Spiritual abuse distorts the heart of faith. It uses God, or the idea of God, as a weapon. It manipulates Scripture, doctrine, or spiritual authority to control, shame, or silence someone. Spiritual abuse is not limited to a certain religion or denomination, and let it be known that abuse in the name of faith is still abuse.

This may look like:
- Mocking or belittling their beliefs
- Preventing someone from practicing their faith
- Using religion to justify mistreatment
- Forcing children into a belief system without a parent's agreement
- Manipulating Scripture to keep someone in the relationship
- Using guilt, shame, or fear of divine punishment to maintain control

Even one form of abuse, whether emotional, physical, or spiritual, can leave lasting scars. Any one of them can shake your sense of safety, distort how you see yourself, and make you wonder if God has turned away. But sometimes, the painful reality is that more than one form of abuse happens at the same time. Emotional manipulation mixed with control, neglect coupled with cruel words, or betrayal tied to spiritual pressure, can deepen the wound and make healing feel even harder.

Sometimes the truth only becomes clear in hindsight, when the red flags you once overlooked finally come into focus. Staying longer than was safe, loving deeply despite the pain, and carrying the weight of a shattered heart can leave anyone wondering if it was their fault, or if healing and wholeness are even possible.

If that's you, let me speak to you clearly and directly: It was not your fault. You didn't cause the abuse, you didn't deserve the pain, and you are not defined by what someone else chose to do to you. Your pain doesn't mean you're weak or beyond repair. It simply means the weight you've been carrying has been unbearably heavy. And yet, here you are, still standing, still seeking, and still hoping for healing. That kind of resilience is a testimony in itself. There's no shame in not seeing it sooner, and there is no guilt in wanting to love and be loved. That desire is not your weakness; it's part of your beautiful, God-given humanity.

Abuse thrives in silence and confusion. But healing begins the moment you name what happened. You are not what was done to you. You are who you choose to become next.

So take a deep breath and begin to let the shame fall away. Let this moment be the turning point and the place where what once felt like an ending becomes a new beginning. You are no longer merely surviving; you are stepping boldly into strength, wrapped in grace, grounded in truth, and surrounded by a love that will never leave you. You are not alone.

Let this be your beginning, not your end.

Your Page to Write: Where Healing Meets Action

1. Take a Moment to Pause and Breathe
Release the weight of blame you've been carrying.

2. Write a Letter to Your Past Self
This letter isn't meant to be sent; it's a gift of grace. Write to the version of yourself who stayed too long, missed the red flags, or now carries shame. Speak gently, truthfully, and without judgment.

3. Share What You Know Now
Remind yourself in that letter that believing the best in someone isn't a weakness. It's a sign of a tender, hopeful heart.

4. Identify One Lie You've Believed About the Abuse
Then, replace it with the truth. For example:
1. Lie: "I should have known better."
2. Truth: "I believed the best because I love deeply. That's not a flaw, it's a gift."

5. Take One Small Symbolic Action to Release That Lie

This could be tearing up a note with the lie written on it, lighting a candle, saying a prayer, or stepping outside to breathe deeply and say aloud: *"It was not my fault. I'm not stuck there anymore."*

WHERE IS GOD IN THE PAIN?

As you begin to walk this path of healing, a natural question often follows: *Where is God in all this? Where was He when it hurt the most?* Understanding abuse, especially when you're in the middle of it, isn't easy. It's confusing, disorienting, and often full of questions that feel impossible to answer. The truth is that victims are rarely targeted because they're weak. More often, they're targeted because they're kind, trusting, hopeful, and because they haven't yet learned what red flags to look for. If these words resonate with your story, please know in your heart that you are not stupid, and you are not beyond healing or hope. You are human, and your heart was made for love, not for harm.

So here's the hope I want to offer: You don't have to figure this out on your own.

Wherever you are in your healing journey, whether you're still in the thick of pain or just beginning to feel light breaking through, you're not alone. I may not know your name or your story, but I know what it feels like to walk through the valley. And while I won't pretend to have all the answers, I can tell you that God has taken the ugliest parts of my story and begun to weave them into something meaningful, something beautiful, and something worth sharing.

Maybe you've wrestled with the same question I once did: *If God is really good, why did He let this happen to me.*

I used to hate it when people tried to answer that with clichés. "Everything happens for a reason," they'd say. Or worse, "God gives His toughest battles to His strongest soldiers." But I don't buy that. I don't believe God hands out trauma like tests. What I *do* believe is that God can take the brokenness this world throws at us and form something powerful in its place. He doesn't give us pain, but He refuses to waste it. He creates warriors not by avoiding the battle, but by walking with us *through* it. Hebrews 13:5 reminds us, *"Never will I leave you; never will I forsake you."*

To understand why suffering exists, we have to go back to the beginning in Genesis. When God created the world, everything was *very good* (Genesis 1:31). The earth was whole, safe, and free from pain. Humanity walked in perfect relationship with God, with each other, and with all creation. But then, in Genesis 3, something shifted. The enemy slithered in, sowing seeds of doubt, deception, and rebellion. That one act of disobedience fractured the perfect world and brought brokenness like abuse, betrayal, fear, and trauma into the story.

This brokenness is not from God. It was never His design. But even when sin entered, God didn't walk away. He stayed close to His creation, promising hope and redemption. Psalm 34:18 tells us, *"The Lord is close to the brokenhearted and saves those who are crushed in spirit."* God doesn't delight in your pain. He doesn't turn a blind eye to injustice. He weeps with you. He fights for you. He heals what others tried to destroy. And He promises that one day, He will make *all* things right.

So if you've ever wondered where God was when it hurt the most, I invite you to keep reading. I believe the next pages might help you see where He has been *all* along.

Why Would God Allow Me to Suffer?

At the heart of this struggle is a tension I've wrestled with deeply: How much control does God have over what happens to us, and how much freedom do we have as human beings?

Some Christian traditions emphasize free will, the idea that God has given us real choices, even when those choices bring pain or suffering. I believe this is how God relates to us, because love is only meaningful when it's freely given and received. As 1 John 4:8 reminds us, *"God is love."* Love that is forced cannot possibly be genuine.

Like many kids, I loved playing "the floor is lava". You know, the game where you leap from couch to couch, trying not to touch the ground. My siblings and I loved turning our living room into an obstacle course despite my parents repeatedly warning us not to do it. One day, when my parents weren't looking, I was fully immersed in this lava adventure. But all of a sudden, I took a leap, missed, and fell face-first into a glass coffee table. I cracked my chin open and ended up in the hospital getting stitches. Ouch!

Before you start feeling sorry for me, let me be clear: I knew the risks going in. I'd been warned more than once, and I still chose to play. But imagine if my mom had been in the room, watching, fully aware of what could happen, but chose not to step in. Would that make it her fault that I got hurt? Of course not. She would've simply allowed me to make my own choice, even if it meant I might get hurt. Not because she didn't care, but because she trusted me to learn from it.

That's a small but powerful picture of how God relates to us. He doesn't force us to stay on the couch. He gives us the freedom to jump, even when He knows we might fall. And while He doesn't cause our pain, He allows our choices, because love without freedom isn't love at all. Still, He never steps out of the room. He's there when we crash, He's there when the brokenness leaves scars, and He's the one who stitches us up again. Even in our worst decisions, even when we land face-first in our own mess, God doesn't turn away. He draws near. He redeems the pain and uses it, not to shame us, but to shape us into people who are wiser, more compassionate, and more dependent on Him.

However, other traditions and denominations emphasize God's absolute sovereignty, His control over all things, including our decisions. This raises difficult questions, such as: *If God is sovereign, does He command suffering? Does He just allow trauma and abuse to happen?*

To be honest, there are no easy answers. For centuries, people of faith have struggled to understand how God's goodness and control fit alongside the pain and evil we experience. Some find comfort in trusting in the mystery of God's plan, knowing His wisdom is far beyond what we can grasp (Isaiah 55:8-9). Others hold onto the hope that even the deepest suffering is part of a larger story, one of healing and restoration that God is weaving together (Romans 8:28).

But here's what I've learned: leaning too far on one side of this debate can cause us to miss the fullness of who God is. If we focus only on God's control, it can make Him seem distant, or worse, like the source and author of our pain. That perspective can make it harder to grasp His loving, tender heart, which freely gives us the gift of choice. But if we emphasize free will alone, we risk imagining God as powerless or uninvolved, watching from afar without a plan or purpose.

The truth, I believe, is that God holds these characteristics in perfect balance. He is sovereign over all things, yet He grants us real freedom, because love without freedom isn't truly love. He's intimately involved in our lives, never forcing, never abandoning, but walking with us through every fall, every scar, and every step toward healing. When we hold both God's power and His loving freedom together, we see a God who is both mighty and merciful, one who holds us close even in the darkest moments and promises to redeem every broken piece. Whether you lean toward free will or divine sovereignty, the heartbeat of Scripture remains: God's love is steadfast, His presence unshakable, and His hope unending.

Where Is God in the Midst of It?

It's only human to ask, *Where is God when I'm hurting? How could He possibly be present in this pain?* If you've ever wrestled with these questions, you're not alone. I've been there too. And it's okay to ask. God welcomes our questions. He's not shaken by our doubt, nor distant in our suffering. Even Jesus, in His darkest hour on the cross, cried out, *"My God, my God, why have you forsaken me?"* (Matthew 27:46). At first, it might sound like abandonment, but the full story of Scripture reminds us that nothing, not even death, can separate us from God's love

(Romans 8:37-39).

God can handle the rawness of our heartbreak, but are we willing to be that vulnerable and to lay it all before Him? He already knows our pain, even before we find the words to say it. After my relationship ended, I was swallowed by darkness. I couldn't see hope or healing; I was lost in desperation. Months passed before I finally realized what had happened to me, and even then, healing felt impossibly slow. I was stuck, broken, and desperate. I turned to God, not from strength, but from pure need.

If someone had told me then that I'd someday be married to a man of God and writing this very book, speaking to women walking through their own storms, I would have laughed. I simply couldn't imagine a future beyond the pain. But God could. He was already weaving a new story out of the wreckage, a story of healing, redemption, and hope. I don't know what He will call you to do with your story, but I believe with every fiber of my being that He will use it for good. What once tried to break you doesn't have to define you.

After Jesus was crucified, He was glorified. And even that wasn't the end; it was the beginning of something eternal. His suffering was not God's absence, but the ultimate proof of His love. Our suffering, as painful and confusing as it is, can become the place where God meets us, reshapes us, and redeems us.

The Bible doesn't avoid pain; it speaks honestly about suffering and how God patiently waits for us to turn to Him. Pain can crush us, or it can be the pathway to healing. Joni Eareckson Tada, who became a quadriplegic after a diving accident as a teenager and has spent decades testifying to God's grace despite immense suffering, put it this way: "God sometimes permits what He hates to accomplish what He loves."[4] Even when we can't see it, Romans 8:28 promises, *"And we know that in all things God works for the good of those who love him, who have been called according to his purpose."*

Right now, your pain may feel like a tangled mess with no clear design. But if you've ever crocheted or watched someone do it, you know that from the back, it looks like chaotic knots, loose ends, and no order. But when you flip it over, the front reveals a beautiful, intentional pattern. Your life is exactly like that. From your view, it may feel messy and meaningless. But God, the Master Designer, sees the whole picture, and one day, you will too.

So where is God in the middle of your abuse, your confusion, and your sorrow? He's closer than you think. When you can't see His hand, trust His heart. He will never leave you or forsake you. And when you feel weakest, when you have nothing left to give, that's when His strength shines brightest. His power is made perfect in our weakness (2 Corinthians 12:9-10). Rest in that truth.

Your Page to Write: Where Healing Meets Action

1. Give Yourself Permission to Ask the Hard Questions

Write them down, whether in a journal, on your phone, or on a scrap of paper. Questions like: *Where was God when it hurt? Why did this happen? Will I ever understand?* Bring your doubts into the light, knowing that God welcomes your honesty. He wants your real, raw heart.

2. Respond With Faith, Even If You Don't Have All the Answers

Try writing a simple response beside your questions. It doesn't need to be perfect or complete, just a statement of trust, such as: *"I may not understand it all, but I believe God is good and was with me even when I couldn't see Him."*

3. Reflect On Your Own "Glass Table" Moment

Take time to reflect on the moments you were hurt. Instead of shame, ask yourself: *What might God be doing through this?* Write one sentence of truth you can hold onto, like: *"This pain has a purpose, and I am not beyond redemption."*

4. Seek Support from Trusted Sources

Reach out to pastors, counselors, or spiritual mentors who can walk alongside you as you wrestle with these questions. Sometimes, hearing God's truth through others who care can bring clarity and comfort. Don't hesitate to ask for prayer and guidance.

5. Dive Into Scripture on Your Own Terms

Look for passages that speak to suffering, God's presence, and hope. Verses like Psalm 34:18, Romans 8:28, and Isaiah 55:8-9 are a good place to start. Let your questions lead you deeper into God's Word as you seek your own answers and reassurance.

6. Declare Your Trust Out Loud

Take a deep breath and say: *"Even when I can't see the pattern, I trust the Designer."* Let this be your anthem for today, a choice to hold onto trust, even in the unknown.

WORSHIP WHEN IT HURTS

"The deepest level of worship is praising God in spite of pain, thanking Him during trials, surrendering while suffering, and loving Him when He seems distant." [5] —Rick Warren

I spent a long time running from my circumstances, from the pain, and if I'm honest, from the presence of God. Suffering had stripped me bare. Heartbreak, trauma, confusion, and grief left me questioning everything I thought I knew about who God was and how He works. I didn't want to pray. I didn't want to sing. I wanted to disappear. But somewhere in the middle of my hiding, I stumbled into worship—not the polished kind, but the raw, desperate kind. And there, in the very place I least expected, I found Him. I found a God who doesn't run from brokenness but meets us in it. I discovered that there is something deeply holy about worshiping in the midst of pain. That even when we're too weak to stand, worship is where we remember we're not alone.

A few years ago, I wrote a song called "YHWH." The title comes from the ancient name of God, Yahweh. It is a name so sacred that Hebrew tradition often left it unspoken. Some scholars say this name even mirrors the sound of our breathing: "Yah" on the inhale, "weh" on the exhale. That means every breath we take, whether we believe in Him or not, is a quiet acknowledgment of His name. We carry His presence with us in every rise and fall of our lungs, and what an incredible truth that is.

When I wrote that song, I was in a place of total brokenness.

I remember sitting on my bedroom floor with tears streaming down my face, barely able to form words. In that moment, all I could do was worship. I cried out to God with what little strength I had, and I sensed Him speak this gently to my heart: "Just breathe. Hear my name in your breath. If you can still call on my name, I'm not finished with you yet." That whisper became the chorus of my song and a lifeline to hold onto in the days that followed.

Wrestling with God: Doubt, Anger, and Faith

Building on the truth that God is present amidst our pain and working even in the brokenness, worship becomes a powerful response. It is not only something that we do after healing, but can be the very way we encounter God in the middle of the hurt. There's something transformative about worshiping through the pain, not after it's passed, not once the healing is complete, but right in the middle of it. Worship reorients our perspective. It lifts our eyes from our circumstances and sets them on the One who is bigger than the storm. It moves us from a posture of panic to a posture of surrender. In my own life, I've noticed that my heart is most desperate for God's presence when I'm hurting. And once you've tasted the joy that comes from worshiping Him, nothing else truly satisfies.

But I want to be honest here. There are seasons when worship feels like the hardest thing to do. When doubt creeps in, anger burns hot, and spiritual dryness leaves us feeling far from God. Maybe you've found yourself asking, *Where are You, God? Why does this hurt so much? How can You let this happen?* These questions don't mean your faith is failing. They mean you're wrestling with God, just like the psalmists who cried out in confusion and pain.

In those wilderness moments, when prayers feel like whispers into an empty room and God seems silent, worship isn't about faking joy or pretending everything is okay. It's about bringing your raw, honest heart to Him anyway, breathing His name even when your voice shakes, and offering your doubts, anger, and silence as a kind of worship that's real and brave.

When we worship through those hard emotions, we choose to fix our eyes on the One who is bigger than our questions, who invites us to wrestle and stay close, instead of running away. Often, it is in that wrestling that our faith deepens, and our worship becomes more authentic than ever before. So if you're in a place of spiritual dryness or overwhelming hurt, know you are not alone. God meets us there, not with condemnation, but with open arms. Let your doubts and broken whispers be part of your worship journey, because worship isn't only for the mountaintops, it's for the valleys too.

Here's the beautiful part: This side of eternity is the only time we get to choose worship in the midst of pain. When we stand before God in heaven, there will be no more suffering or heartbreak. Worship will be the natural response to the beauty of Jesus. But here and now, we have the sacred opportunity to *choose* Him when it's hard. We get to lift our hands when they feel too heavy. We get to sing through tears. That's a kind of worship we'll never get to offer again.

Choosing Worship When It's Hardest

But maybe you're reading this and thinking, *I'm not there yet.*

My pain is too heavy to sing through. I understand, trust me. I want to invite you to look at one of the most powerful moments of faith in Scripture: the story of the woman who had been bleeding for twelve years (Luke 8:43-44). She was tired. Isolated. Labeled "unclean." She had spent everything she had on doctors who couldn't help her. She knew what it was to suffer, not just physically, but emotionally and socially. Still, she reached out, quietly and desperately, to touch the edge of Jesus's robe. And in that moment, she was healed.

What's even more beautiful than the healing is Jesus's response. He turns to face the woman, calls her daughter, and offers her peace. He doesn't just fix her body, He restores her identity. That's what worship does. When we reach out through the pain and when we fall at His feet with nothing left to offer but our brokenness, He meets us there. We may not always be healed the way we hope, but we are always seen, always known, and always loved.

Worship becomes our offering in these moments. It's not about the words we say or the songs we sing; it's about turning toward God even when we don't understand. It's about trusting His heart when we can't trace His hand. That kind of worship takes faith. Real, raw, tested faith.

Psalm 56:8 tells us that God keeps track of all our sorrows, bottles every tear, and records them in His book. Not a single drop of our pain goes unnoticed by the God of the Universe. Doesn't that just leave you in awe? The truth is, sometimes our tears are prayers. Sometimes our breath is our worship. And sometimes, just sitting in His presence is the most powerful declaration of trust we can make.

So if all you can do right now is breathe, then breathe. Speak His name with every inhale and exhale. Trust in the truth that He's not finished with you yet. When you worship in the middle of your pain, you declare that your faith is not dependent on your circumstances. You proclaim that even here, even now, God is still worthy.

As you turn the page and continue this journey, I pray you begin to believe that worship isn't just what you do, it's who you are becoming. One breath, one step, and one act of trust at a time.

Your Page to Write: Where Healing Meets Action

1. Pause and Make Space for Yourself

Find a quiet moment today, wherever you are, to stop and take a few intentional, slow breaths. This is your time to connect, even if just for a moment.

2. Breathe in God's Name

As you inhale deeply, quietly say or think the name *Yahweh*. Start with the "Yah." Feel God's presence coming in with each breath.

3. Breathe Out in Trust

As you exhale slowly, say or think "weh." Let this breath remind you that God's presence never leaves you. It is with you through every struggle and every moment of pain.

4. Offer Your Emotions to God

If you feel able, bring your feelings of doubt, anger, confusion, or even hope before Him. Offer these emotions honestly as your act of worship. You don't need perfect words or "right" feelings; simply bring your heart.

5. Let Your Breath Be Your Prayer

Continue breathing with this rhythm of "Yah" as you inhale, "weh" as you exhale. Let your breath become your prayer, your refuge, and your connection to God today.

6. Return to This Practice Whenever You Need to

Remember, this simple prayer is always available to you. Whenever pain or uncertainty feels overwhelming, come back to these breaths and let them ground you in God's presence.

SET APART TO BE MADE WHOLE

"Look for yourself and you will find loneliness and despair. But look for Christ and you will find Him and everything else." [6] —*C.S. Lewis*

Think back to those strange, silent months at the height of the COVID-19 pandemic, when the whole world seemed to hold its breath. Schools shut down. Workplaces went dark. Birthday parties, graduations, weddings, and even funerals vanished from calendars. Toilet paper flew off the shelves as fear flooded the grocery aisles. But beyond the chaos, something even heavier settled in: isolation. Mothers gave birth alone in sterile rooms. The elderly spent their final moments without a single hand to hold. The sick were sealed off behind hospital doors. If you lived through that season, you know it wasn't just inconvenient. It was deeply and painfully lonely. The data confirmed what hearts already knew: Loneliness had become its own kind of pandemic.

For me, COVID-19 hit during my junior year of high school and lasted through my entire senior year. Like many others, I felt that loneliness. Almost immediately after the world shut down, my dating life did too. My two-year relationship ended on painful terms, and everything I had built my life around was flipped upside down. I had lost the person I had centered my world around for the last two years, I couldn't see my friends, and I wasn't able to go anywhere to distract myself from the heartbreak. Soon, a string of health issues added to my isolation, and out of fear of getting the virus, I was placed on an even stricter lockdown.

But despite the challenges and loneliness, that season turned out to be one of the greatest gifts I could have ever received. In that isolation, I turned to God, and He met me in the broken places I didn't even know needed healing. My loneliness wasn't a death sentence; it was a doorway. It became a sacred invitation for growth, healing, and deeper intimacy with God.

Yet even as worship became a lifeline in that pain, there were moments when the songs slowed, the tears dried, and a heavy silence settled in. Worship in the middle of pain is powerful, but sometimes, the weight of loneliness leaves us without words or melodies. In those quiet spaces, when worship feels too hard and God's voice seems distant, loneliness can press deeply into our souls.

Even then, God is not far away. He's waiting in the stillness, inviting us into a new kind of closeness, a quiet aloneness with Him that holds our hurting hearts when words fail. This journey through pain isn't only about lifting our voices; it's also about learning to rest fully in His presence when the isolation overwhelms us.

If you're reading this and carrying the heavy weight of loneliness and wondering if God has abandoned you, I want to assure you: He hasn't. But don't just take my word for it. Take God's. Deuteronomy 31:8 says, *"The Lord himself goes before you and will be with you; He will never leave you nor forsake you. Do not be afraid; do not be discouraged."* You've probably heard that God is with you and has a plan for your life a thousand times. And that's still true. But maybe you're still stuck wondering, *What could possibly be God's purpose in leaving me all alone right now?*

Why God Allows Seasons of Separation

God allows seasons of separation for four main reasons. First, He uses this time to equip us with what we need for what lies ahead. During COVID, God had to re-teach me how to trust Him, how to be vulnerable with Him, how to rely on Him alone, and how to listen for His voice again. I desperately needed life to slow down so I could refocus on what truly matters. That slowing down turned into a blessing that I'm beyond grateful for.

When I was in middle school, we had to do a team-building exercise where one person was blindfolded and the other had to guide them through the school using only verbal instructions. The goal wasn't just to listen, it was to learn to recognize and trust the voice leading you. Without that trust, you might easily end up walking straight into a wall or a pole. That experience taught me something important: Hearing a voice is one thing, but truly trusting it, especially when you can't see, is what keeps you safe and moving forward.

The second reason God allows seasons of separation is much like that exercise. He uses these times to train us to recognize and trust His voice above all the noise in our lives. The enemy's goal is to drown out God's voice, but sometimes God intentionally lowers the volume around us, away from friends, mentors, family, and even our own internal chatter, so we can learn to hear Him clearly. In these seasons, we are being taught to listen carefully, to discern His guidance apart from everything else, and to trust Him even when it feels quiet or uncomfortable.

Third, He separates us so we can give Him our full attention.

When our attention is undivided, God can heal wounds the world cannot touch. I'm sure if my breakup hadn't happened during COVID, I would've filled the hole in my heart with distraction after distraction. But forced into isolation, I healed in a way that was permanent, not just a temporary fix.

Finally, God separates us so that when we emerge from loneliness, we are unrecognizable to those who once knew us only by our wounds. Instead of being defined by heartbreak or loss, we become known by the love and joy of our Father.

So what if you haven't been abandoned at all? What if you've actually been placed strategically into a season of isolation to receive an eternal comfort rather than a temporary one?

That's the heart of this journey: moving from loneliness to *aloneness* with God.

Because the true gift of these seasons isn't just what God prepares in us or how He shapes us, it's His presence that meets us in the quiet, the pain, and the waiting. It's in the stillness that He draws close, inviting us into a hidden place where we can find peace, healing, and hope that no one else can give. This sacred aloneness with God is where transformation happens, and new life begins.

Alone with God: Finding Hidden Peace and Hope

In this season of isolation, God is sanctifying you and shaping you to look more like Him. Your thoughts, ambitions, and desires will begin to shift. Loneliness can be a gift because it forces us to stop relying on what people can't provide. And to be honest, you can't cure loneliness without a healthy relationship with God. When your relationship with Him is secure, every other relationship is strengthened. And when those relationships break, you still have a firm place to stand.

Loneliness can be a beautiful thing because it gives us a glimpse into what Jesus felt. He experienced loneliness on the cross. He felt abandoned by His closest friends. When a woman poured oil on Him, others mocked Him as unworthy. When He asked His disciples to stay awake and pray, they fell asleep. When we understand loneliness as a way to share in Jesus's experience, we begin to see a strange kind of beauty in it. Taking your loneliness to Jesus means He meets you with understanding and compassion. And that same Jesus, the One who rose from the grave, knows every ache inside you and loves you still.

Ultimately, God sometimes allows us to experience loneliness so that we can learn the difference between being alone and being alone *with Him*. Loneliness can feel empty, painful, and isolating, but aloneness with God is a sacred place of presence and peace. In that hidden space, it's just you and Him. There, you find rest as God covers you with the shadow of His wings, just as Psalm 91 describes. Your walk with the Lord deepens because your focus is fully on Him. He speaks to you. He protects you. He heals you. He holds you close, like a Father carrying His child.

Take heart and trust that God will bring the right people into your life in His perfect timing. But for now, we must choose obedience and perseverance in the waiting. God will not leave you in your loneliness. And when you finally reach the next chapter of your life, you'll look back and see His fingerprints on every page. You'll realize this wasn't a detour, it was a holy invitation.

Your Page to Write: Where Healing Meets Action

1. Find a Quiet Moment Today

Set aside some time to be alone with your thoughts, away from distractions. Create a peaceful space where you can reflect honestly.

2. Reflect on Your Current Season

Think about where you are right now, especially if you're feeling lonely or isolated. What emotions or thoughts come up? Write them down to bring clarity to your experience.

3. Notice God's Work in Your Life

Look for ways you sense God is equipping you, shaping your character, or inviting you to trust Him more deeply during this season. Jot down these signs of His presence and purpose.

4. Choose One Simple Way to Connect With God This Week

This might be a prayer, journaling your feelings, or reading a comforting Scripture like Psalm 62:5-8, that speaks to your heart.

5. Make This Your Intentional Step Toward God

Commit to this small practice as a way of embracing solitude, not as loneliness, but as sacred time with God.

6. Remember God's Promise

Hold onto the truth that He is always with you and will never leave you, even in moments of solitude.

PART TWO

The Pages That Embrace Grace

BELOVED, NOT BROKEN

"The more deeply we reinforce our identity in Christ, the more fortified we will be against the onslaught of opposing voices in our lives." [7]
—*Steven Furtick*

I was only eleven when the way I saw myself began to fracture.

I had just started sixth grade, still in training bras and Justice t-shirts, when a mistrusted family friend asked if I was "ready to shop at Victoria's Secret." It wasn't really a question. It was the moment my body became a conversation, an object to be sexualized. Every photo of me from then on became a dissection—what parts of me were "developing," what parts needed to change, to shrink, to fit someone else's idea of beauty. I was just a little girl, trying to find my place in the world, trying to figure out who I was while the world was already deciding who I should be.

A few years later, I found myself in a relationship with my abuser. For two long years, I was called everything but my name. It started subtly with pet names and praise, but quickly turned into a daily storm of verbal beatings. "Ugly." "Fat." "Stupid." "Worthless." "Undeserving of love." "Broken." Every word wasn't just spoken—it was weaponized. They didn't just hurt; they hollowed me out. Slowly, I began to believe them. Piece by piece, insult by insult, I was stripped down until I could barely recognize the girl beneath the shame. Just a shell. Just silence. Just survival.

From then on, I spent years believing I was only as worthy as the last person who walked away. I carried the belief that I was hard to love and grossly unattractive. I tried to measure my value by someone else's approval, attention, or affection. The words haunted me. I felt like I was wearing a name tag that read "unlovable" or "too broken." I felt like everyone saw it and believed it as much as I did. That's the thing about abuse. It doesn't just hurt in the moment; it leaves a messy residue. They try to rename us, and oftentimes, it works.

I'll be honest, healing didn't happen all at once. There wasn't a single moment when everything "changed." Instead, it was a thousand little moments when God whispered a different identity over me. He began to show me that I wasn't what had been done to me, but rather what Christ had done *for* me. Slowly, I began to question if maybe I wasn't what they said. Maybe I wasn't what *he* said. Maybe I am more than the broken pieces left shattered. It took time to hear God. It took even longer to believe Him. But slowly, the truth began to rise above the lies. I thought I was too far gone and too damaged to be called worthy again, but my Maker never stopped calling me by my real name: *Chosen. Beloved. Redeemed.*

Renamed by Grace: God's Truth Over Our Lies

Healing began the moment I realized that the names thrown at me were not the ones I was created to carry. Truth be told, God isn't in the business of reusing the world's labels. He is rewriting, reworking, and renaming us. That's what God does. He doesn't just patch up the broken parts; He renames them. Over time, I began to trade in the lies I had believed for the truth of who I am in Christ. But not all at once, and not without constant struggle.

You see, the enemy had me right where he wanted me, and so did my abuser. Abusers love to see us broken and ashamed because it makes them feel as if they have power, control, and victory over us. Similarly, the enemy loves to see us scared, broken, and hidden in shame. Because when we sit in that space, we tend to run from the presence of God. It's so easy for our shame to keep us from God's grace, yet the whole purpose of grace is to cover our shame. In His kindness, God takes off every false label and replaces it with something holy and new.

We're not the first people the Lord has done this for. In fact, renaming is one of God's favorite methods of restoration and healing. In Scripture, God repeatedly gives new names to people He's about to do something new through. When God is about to call them into something greater, deeper, and more aligned with His heart, He grants a new name. Abram was renamed Abraham, which means "father of many nations," before he ever held his own child in his arms. Sarai became Sarah, which means "princess," an identity rooted in God's promise, rather than her barrenness (Genesis 17). Jacob, whose name meant deceiver, wrestled with God and was renamed Israel, which means "God contends." He was no longer defined by his past but by his encounter with the Lord (Genesis 32). Simon, the impulsive fisherman, was renamed Peter, which means "rock." He wasn't renamed for who he was in that moment, but for who Jesus knew He would become (Matthew 16).

Finally, there's Saul. This was a man who persecuted the church with violence and power. He encountered the risen Christ on a dusty road and was renamed (Acts 13). Christ gave him the name Paul, and he went on to become a humble servant, missionary, and author of much of the New Testament. Each of these people was given labels. They had stories, reputations, sins, shame, and regret. Yet God chose to write more for their stories. And He's writing more for yours. We don't have to be defined by what's done to us or even what's been done *by* us. God gives us a new name. Not because we've earned it, but because He is redeeming us. Redeeming you.

For so long, I believed I was what they said I was: "too much," "not enough," "broken," "unworthy," "hard to love." But slowly and gently, God began to speak different names over me—not ones of shame, but of restoration. I didn't always hear an audible voice. I heard Him through Scripture, worship, and in quiet moments when I dared to ask, "God, who do you say I am?" I began to hear it: *Beloved. Chosen. Beautiful. Intentional. Whole. Mine.* It wasn't instant, and it didn't always feel true. But the more I pursued God and opened my heart to His voice, the more those new names started to stick.

I started to truly believe the new identity Christ was speaking over me. I wasn't unwanted—I was handpicked and pursued. I wasn't broken—I was being made whole. I wasn't too far gone—I was already brought near. I wasn't buried in shame—I was washed clean by the blood of Christ. The truth is, you are...

Beloved – Isaiah 43:4

Chosen – John 15:16

Redeemed – Ephesians 1:7

A New Creation – 2 Corinthians 5:17

A Child of God – 1 John 3:1

A Friend of God – John 15:15

Free – John 8:36

Forgiven – Ephesians 1:7

Healed – 1 Peter 2:24

Clean – 1 Corinthians 6:11

Beautifully and Wonderfully Made – Psalm 139:14

God's Masterpiece – Ephesians 2:10

More than a Conqueror – Romans 8:37

Victorious – 1 Corinthians 15:57

Walking in a New Identity and Choosing Truth Daily

Learning to walk in your God-given name rather than your trauma-given name is not a one-time event. It's a daily decision. Even after I knew the truth, even after I could recite verses and speak the names God had given me, I still had days when I felt like an imposter wearing a crown too big for my head. I could say, "I'm beloved," but still feel unwanted. I could read "redeemed" but still remember what I did or what was done to me. That's the thing about healing ... it's holy, but it's also incredibly hard. You have to unlearn years of lies and intentionally replace them with the truth of God's Word.

For me, healing didn't come easily. When I was deep in therapy, wrestling with the weight of something called post-traumatic stress disorder (PTSD), my therapist gave me an assignment. I was stuck, struggling to speak the truth of what had happened to me, unable to piece the fragments together. She gently challenged me: *Write your story.*

That terrified me. Putting it on paper would make it real ... the pain, the confusion, the trauma. It would live outside of me, where I couldn't pretend it wasn't there. For weeks, I avoided it. I told myself I wasn't ready. But eventually, I picked up a journal and started to write.

And suddenly, there I was scattered across the pages. Raw. Messy. Wounded. I saw the names I had taken on, names my abuser had etched into my identity. Names like "unworthy," "too much," "used," "invisible." I didn't even realize I had been carrying them until I saw them written down in ink.

But one day, something shifted. I felt the Spirit nudge me to list every label I had accepted as truth. So I did. Then, on the next page of that same journal, I opened my Bible and began writing what God says about me next to each one.

Daughter. Forgiven. Pure. Whole. Valued.

As I wrote these holy names, I began to cross out the lies one by one. And the tears came. Every step toward those true names was a step away from shame. It didn't always feel like freedom, but it was.

Sometimes, freedom looks like trembling hands holding a pen. Sometimes, it looks like worshiping through tears because, for the first time, you actually believe God isn't disgusted with you. It looks like choosing His voice when the old ones still echo. Healing meant refusing to agree with the names my past gave me and finally embracing the names God had spoken over me all along.

What to Do When the Old Names Return

If you've ever walked the road of healing, you know it's rarely a straight path. A few months after I was diagnosed with PTSD, I wanted a tangible and visual reminder of my journey, a way to hold onto truth when panic or old lies resurfaced. For me, it took the form of an illustration of a heartbeat EKG line woven with flowers and thorns, and the words: "Growth is not linear." It wasn't just a drawing; it was a declaration. I needed the reminder for the days when panic came back like a wave, when the old names resurfaced and whispered lies that I thought I had silenced. I needed to remember this isn't failure. This isn't going backward. This is healing, and healing takes time.

There are days when it feels like you're starting all over again. And there are days when you don't even think about the trauma. Both are part of the journey. That illustration became a marker for me, a visual sign of the truth that no matter what kind of day it is, God still gave me breath. A heartbeat. Life. Which means He's not done with me. He's not done redeeming.

It's been nearly five years since my trauma, and still, shame tries to creep in like a shadow. Sometimes it's a memory. Sometimes it's a comment that cuts deeper than it should. And suddenly, I hear the old names rise again: *Broken. Too much. Not enough. Hard to love.*

But here's what I'm learning: Just because the old names show up doesn't mean I have to wear them like a label. They don't belong to me anymore. When the old names return, and they will, I've learned to run straight to the Source. I open the Word and anchor myself in what is written, not just what is felt. I speak Scripture out loud, even when my emotions haven't caught up. I reach out to people I trust, those who will pray over me, remind me who I am, and speak life when I forget.

Because this isn't just emotional; it's spiritual warfare. And the weapon? Truth. You must fight lies with light. You must fight shame with Scripture. You must fight fear with the voice of the Father.

So when those familiar accusations start creeping in, don't panic. Don't spiral. Don't give them space to settle. Remember this: The enemy doesn't waste energy on things that don't matter. If he's attacking your identity, it's because your identity in Christ threatens him. And that truth alone should tell you how powerful your story *really* is.

You are not what was done to you. You are not who they said you were. You are not too broken, too dirty, or too damaged. You are not a mistake. You are not beyond repair. You are who God says you are. And He says you are loved, you are seen, you are known, you are healed, you are whole, and you are *His*. If you walk away from this chapter with anything, let it be this: You don't have to answer to names that Heaven never gave you. *You've been renamed.*

So write it down. Say it aloud. Pray it through tears. Live like it's true, even on the days it doesn't feel true yet. Because over time, truth wins. Healing comes. And you'll begin to walk not as a victim, not as an impostor, but as a daughter of the King, wearing the name He gave you from the beginning: *Beloved.*

Your Page to Write: Where Healing Meets Action

1. Write Down the Negative Names or Labels

Take a moment to list the hurtful words or identities the world or your trauma has placed on you. Be honest and thorough. These might be things like "unlovable," "broken," or "worthless."

2. Search the Bible for God's Truth

Using your Bible, look up verses or names that show how God truly sees you. Examples include "beloved" (Song of Solomon 2:4), "fearfully and wonderfully made" (Psalm 139:14), or "child of God" (John 1:12). Write these God-given names or truths next to the lies.

3. Choose One Truth to Focus on This Week

Pick one of God's affirming names or promises that speaks to your heart. Meditate on it daily, speak it out loud, and let it sink deep into your mind and heart.

4. Prepare for Moments When Old Lies Resurface

When those familiar lies creep back in, have a plan: anchor yourself in Scripture, speak God's truth out loud, and reach out to trusted friends, pastors, or counselors who can remind you of your true identity in Christ.

5. Practice This Regularly

Make this exercise a repeated practice, allowing God's truth to gradually reshape your heart and mind.

JESUS AND A THERAPIST

"The Lord is close to the brokenhearted and saves those who are crushed in spirit."— Psalm 34:18

For a long time, I believed that if I just prayed hard enough, read my Bible faithfully, and trusted God deeply, the darkness would all go away. I thought my anxiety would disappear, my triggers would evaporate, and the fog that weighed down my soul would suddenly clear. I believed that if I had enough faith, I wouldn't need help from anyone but Jesus. And if the pain was still there, I must not be a "good enough Christian."

To be completely honest, I still believe Jesus is enough. I believe there is freedom in Christ and healing in His name. I believe He is still in the business of doing miracles. But I also believe that He heals in various ways. I've learned that He often works through people, through doctors, through medication, through licensed counselors and trauma-informed therapists, through friends who show up when we can't speak, through moments of grace that we never expected and help we never thought we were allowed to need.

So this chapter is for those who are scared to ask for help because they think it makes them weak or a "bad Christian." It's for the one who's been told by someone in the church that mental illness is only a "spiritual problem." It's for the one suffering in silence because they believe struggling means they're not trusting God enough. If that's you, I want to say this as clearly and tenderly as I can: There is no shame in seeking help. Not now. Not ever.

Jesus, Therapy, and Medication: Allies in Healing

Struggling with your mental health is not a sin, especially after abuse, trauma, or heartbreak. It's a human response to an inhuman weight. Your anxiety does not disqualify you from God's love. Your depression is not a sign of spiritual failure. It's a signal that your mind, body, and soul are crying out for care, and praise God, He has provided tools for that care. Sometimes, the most spiritual thing you can do is make a counseling appointment. Sometimes it's saying yes to medication that gives your brain room to breathe. Sometimes it's setting boundaries, saying no, or finally telling someone the truth when they ask, "How are you really doing?" These things aren't weak. They're wise. And they might just be the beginning of your breakthrough.

Let me say it clearly: Jesus and therapy are not enemies. Jesus and medication are not rivals. Jesus is the Healer, and He is not offended by the tools that help bring His healing into your daily life. In fact, I believe He delights in your courage to pursue it. We see His heart in Isaiah 61, where the Messiah is described as the One sent *"to bind up the brokenhearted... to comfort all who mourn... to give them a crown of beauty instead of ashes, the oil of joy instead of mourning, and a garment of praise instead of a spirit of despair."* That is emotional restoration. That is soul-deep, life-altering healing. Jesus came for this.

Recognizing and Fighting Spiritual Warfare

All that said, our healing isn't just a physical or emotional journey. It's also a spiritual one. We have a very real enemy who wants to keep us trapped in cycles of shame, fear, and hopelessness. Sometimes, the darkness you're fighting isn't just depression; it's spiritual warfare. Sometimes, the apathy you feel after a spiritual high isn't just burnout; it's the enemy trying to snuff out your fire.

Over the years, I've come to recognize the spiritual attacks on my life for what they are. For example, I had the opportunity to attend the Passion Conference in Atlanta, Georgia, in 2024. While I was there, I felt the Lord reaffirming His calling on my life. I felt on fire for Him, and my spirit was renewed. However, as soon as I got back, I was hit with brain fog, anxiety, and an overall lack of motivation to spend time with God. To make it worse, I felt guilty for feeling that way.

When this happens, the enemy wants you to blame yourself. We often assume our struggles are all our fault, but what if some of them are actually the result of spiritual sabotage? When we begin to grasp that there's an intentional attack on us, we start to see our struggle for what it really is. It's not just emotional fallout. It is a battle.

"The thief comes only to steal and kill and destroy; I have come that they may have life, and have it to the full." – John 10:10

The enemy is strategic. He often comes after your identity, your passions, your thoughts, and even your peace. His lies can sound convincing, like whispers: "You're not good enough," or

"God could never use someone like you." Sometimes the most dangerous lies are the ones that sound almost true.

Just as he tempted Jesus in the wilderness in Matthew 4, the enemy can twist Scripture to confuse and mislead us. He even pulled from God's own words, quoting Psalm 91 to challenge Jesus, saying, *"If you are the Son of God, throw yourself down, for it is written, 'He will command his angels concerning you...'"* He tried to make Jesus doubt His identity, His mission, and God's timing by taking truth out of context. But Jesus met each temptation with Scripture, faithfully and fully. To the hunger-driven challenge, He replied, *"It is written: 'Man shall not live on bread alone, but on every word that comes from the mouth of God'"* (Deuteronomy 8:3). When urged to test God's protection, He responded, *"It is also written: 'Do not put the Lord your God to the test'"* (Deuteronomy 6:16). And when offered worldly power, He said firmly, *"Away from me, Satan! For it is written: 'Worship the Lord your God, and serve him only'"* (Deuteronomy 6:13).

Even today, the enemy works in similar ways, subtly twisting truth, misusing Scripture, and tempting us to question God's love, timing, or purpose. He might whisper, "God is holy, so you must be perfect before He can love you." While it's true that God is holy, the lie is thinking you must earn His love. Or he might say, "God will protect you, so you should never take risks," turning God's faithfulness into fear and hesitation. Sometimes he uses our past mistakes or hurts, saying, "Because this happened, you're unworthy or broken beyond repair."

But here's the truth: Your past may have shaped you, but it does not define you, and it does not cancel God's redeeming work in your life. When we recognize these half-truths and respond with God's Word, just as Jesus did, we guard our hearts, minds, and identity in Him. Then, we step into freedom instead of fear.

God gives us the armor of truth, righteousness, faith, and His Word to fight back (Ephesians 6). That's why healing must happen on all fronts: the physical, emotional, and spiritual. We don't get to ignore the enemy and pretend he doesn't exist, but we also don't live in fear of him because Jesus has already won.

Still, we need to stay alert. That's why counseling, medication, prayer, Scripture, and community all matter. They work together. One isn't a substitute for the other. We don't put our faith in therapists or medication. We put our faith in God only, but we allow God to work as He sees fit through them. We don't pray *instead of going* to therapy; we pray *while* we go. We don't take medication and stop seeking God; we take medication and seek Him all the more.

Healing is both/and. Not either/or.

Come as You Are

The Lord is not far from you. Even when your mind is spinning and your emotions are raw, He is near. And He has given you resources: doctors, counselors, friends, pastors, prayer, Scripture, worship, and yes, even medication. These are not crutches. They are grace.

I remember the first time I sat across from a counselor. I was terrified. I wondered if I would be judged or labeled "too broken." But instead, I was met with kindness, empathy, and truth. That counselor didn't replace Jesus, but she helped me find Him again in the dark. She helped me name my pain and trace it back to its roots. She helped me see that I wasn't crazy; I was hurting. And healing was possible.

Taking medication was a humbling decision too. It gave me just enough breath to begin climbing out of the pit. It wasn't a betrayal of my faith; it was an act of mercy. It steadied me long enough to do the deeper spiritual work that God was calling me to. For me, it was temporary, but I know some may need medication for longer, and that's okay too. My hope is that it isn't used as a crutch to avoid the root of the pain, but as a bridge that helps you gently step toward a healing process that truly addresses and processes what's inside, leaning on God's guidance and love along the way.

"Come to me, all who are weary and burdened, and I will give you rest." — Matthew 11:28

Jesus doesn't say, "Come to me once you've got it all figured out." He just says: Come. Maybe today, that looks like calling a therapist. Maybe it's filling the prescription your doctor recommended. Maybe it's admitting to a trusted friend that you're not okay. That is not weakness, it's courage. It's not a lack of faith, it's faith in action.

And if you've ever been told that needing help makes you less trusting or dependent on the Lord, I want to lovingly break that lie off of you. You are not less than. You are not failing. You are not too far gone. You are deeply, wildly loved by a God who sees you and wants you whole.

"Praise be to the God... who comforts us in all our troubles, so that we can comfort those in any trouble with the comfort we ourselves receive from God."— 2 Corinthians 1:3-4

So whether you're deep in the valley or just now realizing it's okay to ask for help, let this chapter be a nudge to keep going. Keep praying. Keep showing up to therapy. Keep clinging to the truth. Keep pursuing healing on every level: physical, emotional, mental, and spiritual. Jesus is in every part of it. He is the source of all healing, no matter the method. He is the power behind every counselor's wisdom, every medication's relief, every friend's embrace, and every prayer you whisper in the night.

You don't have to choose between faith and help. Choose both.

Your Page to Write: Where Healing Meets Action

1. Choose One Way to Reach Out for Help Today
This could mean scheduling a counseling appointment, filling a prescription for medication, or sharing your struggles with a trusted friend, pastor, or mentor. Taking this step is a sign of strength, not weakness.

2. Commit to Leaning Into Your Faith
Pray for courage and guidance as you take this step. Ask God to be your strength and healer throughout your journey.

3. Read Scripture That Encourages Healing and God's Love

Find verses that remind you of God's presence and restoration, such as Psalm 147:3 or Jeremiah 29:11. Let these truths anchor your heart.

4. Remember That Seeking Help Is an Act of Faith

Know that reaching out isn't failure, it's trusting God with your healing and taking responsibility for your wellbeing.

5. Keep Moving Forward, One Step at a Time

Healing is a journey, not a race. Celebrate each step you take, no matter how small.

OWNING THE HEAING,
NOT THE HURT

"Those who cooperate most fully with forgiveness are those who dance most freely in the beauty of redemption." [8] *– Lysa TerKeurst*

Forgiveness is one of the hardest things to talk about when you've been deeply hurt. You don't just wake up one day and say, "I'm over it." You carry the ache in your body, the memories in your mind, and the anger in your chest. Sometimes, it feels like if you let go, they win.

But hear me on this: Forgiveness isn't saying what they did was okay. It's saying, "I won't let this pain define me anymore." It's how you stop carrying the weight of what they did and begin reclaiming the space they tried to steal from your heart. You don't forgive because they deserve it. You forgive because you deserve peace.

This chapter is about that brave, holy choice to stop rehearsing the hurt and start releasing it. It's about owning your *healing,* not the *hurt.* Not by rushing the process, but by walking with God through every step of it.

And let me be clear before we dive in. Choosing forgiveness does not mean you forfeit your right to seek justice through the law. If what happened to you was criminal, report it. Press charges. Get legal help if that's what you desire. God is not opposed to justice; He is the very author of it. Romans 13 tells us that earthly authorities exist to uphold justice and protect the vulnerable. Forgiveness and accountability can coexist. You can pursue legal action while also pursuing healing. You can set boundaries and still guard your heart from bitterness. One is about consequences; the other is about your own wholeness. And both matter to God.

Love Is Not the Same as Reconnection

When Jesus said in Luke 6:27-28, *"Love your enemies, do good to those who hate you, bless those who curse you, pray for those who mistreat you,"* He wasn't asking you to run back into the arms of someone who hurt you. Many survivors of abuse feel guilt when they read these verses, wondering if loving their abuser means letting them back in. But biblical love doesn't mean silence, submission, or enduring continued harm. Jesus never called us to stay in danger for the sake of "turning the other cheek."

What Jesus is pointing to is a love that begins in your heart. It's the choice not to let hatred, bitterness, or shame take root inside you. It's the gentle surrender of your pain to God instead of carrying it alone. It's not about letting your offender off the hook. It's about letting you off the hook of vengeance, bitterness, and the endless mental replays of what they did. It doesn't make the wrong okay. It doesn't erase what was done. But it opens the door to peace, a way to stop replaying the hurt and finally rest in the knowledge that you are not defined by what was done to you.

Loving in this way becomes a quiet shelter for your heart. It doesn't make you weak; it makes you tender with yourself. It makes space for your soul to breathe and for God's restoration to take root. In the stillness of that love, you find freedom, not because the pain is gone, but because your heart is learning to live beyond it.

God Sees, God Knows, God Judges Justly

You need to know this: God does not take your wounds lightly. He isn't telling you to "get over it" or move on too fast. Psalm 37: 28-29 says, *"For the Lord loves the just and will not forsake his faithful ones. Wrongdoers will be completely destroyed; the offspring of the wicked will perish. The righteous will inherit the land and dwell in it forever."* Jesus isn't asking you to call evil good. He's asking you to trust Him with justice, to step into healing by releasing the toxic weight that bitterness becomes. Releasing doesn't mean forgetting. It doesn't mean denying what happened. It means choosing to live in the freedom Jesus died to give you.

Forgiveness is often misunderstood. Some think it means pretending everything is fine, but that's not true forgiveness. Real forgiveness acknowledges the harm for what it was and still chooses to release its hold on your life. It may mean setting boundaries, even cutting ties for your safety. It may mean walking away and never speaking to them again. But what forgiveness *always* means is freedom from being defined by the harm. You are not what they did to you. You are who God says you are: *whole, beloved, and redeemed.*

Forgiveness Is a Process, Not a Moment

Forgiveness isn't a switch you flip; it's a journey. For many who've been deeply wounded, it doesn't happen in one prayer or journal entry. It often comes in waves. Some days, it feels easier to let go. On others, you feel the sting of what was lost all over again. That doesn't mean you're failing. It means you're human.

God is patient with this process, and you can be too. Forgiveness might begin with a simple, honest prayer: "God, I want to forgive, but I don't know how." That small act of willingness is enough to start. As you give God access to your heart, as you name the hurt and refuse to feed the bitterness, He begins to soften what feels hard. You may still grieve, and you may still feel anger. But little by little, the grip of that pain loosens.

Forgiveness often begins in the quiet courage of facing your pain head-on. That might look like journaling, confiding in someone you trust, or simply pouring your heart out to God. Healing grows from honest acknowledgment. And through it all, you can lean into God's strength, asking Him to help you forgive, even when your heart feels frozen.

You must be gentle with yourself. Healing isn't a straight line, and it's okay to stumble or feel stuck. Surround yourself with support as you navigate this process. Confide in a counselor, a trusted friend, or a faith community. Let God's promises sink in deeply, reminding you that He restores what was lost.

Practice small acts of grace: a quiet prayer, a breath of gratitude, or a moment of peace. These daily steps slowly loosen bitterness's grip. And don't forget to celebrate progress, no matter how small. Every step you take away from pain and toward freedom is a victory. Forgiveness isn't just a destination; it's the path where healing and hope grow stronger with every breath.

God doesn't expect you to forget, minimize, or rush the

process. He invites you to walk with Him through it. He knows how heavy the wound is, and He knows how to carry it with you. And the beautiful thing? Each time you move forward in grace, even when you don't fully feel it, you're stepping closer to freedom. That is forgiveness in motion.

Pray Even When It Feels Impossible

One of the most courageous things you can do is pray for someone who hurt you. Not in a dismissive way, but in a way that says, *"God, I can't, but You can."* Pray that they come to repentance. Pray that they find the healing they need, often the very healing they refused to pursue before they hurt you. And pray that God softens the parts of your heart that are still frozen.

Jesus Himself modeled this on the cross. After being beaten, mocked, abandoned, and crucified, He prayed: *"Father, forgive them, for they do not know what they are doing"* (Luke 23:34). That wasn't weakness. That was a strength rooted in the love of God. Abuse was never God's will for you. But healing is. Freedom is. Redemption is. Your past pain doesn't disqualify you from God's purpose. In fact, He may use the very pain that tried to bury you to plant something that produces life in someone else.

A friend once told me, "You'll know you've forgiven someone when the thought of them in heaven doesn't make you angry anymore." That one sentence convicted me to my core. Forgiveness is one of the hardest things Jesus calls us to, and yet it's also one of the most freeing. His forgiveness has no agenda. It's complete, unearned, and life-giving.

You don't have to go back to what broke you to prove you've forgiven it. Just keep walking forward. That's what forgiveness does: It lets you move. Loving your enemy doesn't mean reentering the battlefield. Sometimes, it means staying far away and praying from a healed place. Sometimes, it looks like therapy. Sometimes, it looks like naming the pain out loud. Sometimes, it looks like just breathing again.

But it *always* looks like Jesus.

Your Page to Write: Where Healing Meets Action

1. Honestly Acknowledge Your Pain

Take time to write down or pray about the hurt you've experienced. Be honest with God about how deeply it has affected you.

2. Release Bitterness and Vengeance to God

Give your anger and desire for revenge over to Him. Ask for His help to forgive, even when it feels impossible.

3. Take Practical Steps to Protect Your Healing

Set healthy boundaries to guard your heart. This might mean limiting contact or creating emotional distance. Remember, forgiveness doesn't mean forcing reconciliation.

4. Practice Daily Acts of Grace

Show kindness and patience to yourself as you heal. If you feel able, extend small acts of grace toward those who hurt you.

5. Remember That Forgiveness is a Process

Be gentle and patient with yourself. Healing takes time, and God's timing is perfect.

FEAR WILL NOT HAVE
THE FINAL WORD

"So do not fear, for I am with you; do not be dismayed, for I am your God. I will strengthen you and help you; I will uphold you with my righteous right hand." – Isaiah 41:10

When I was little, I spent many sleepless nights wide awake, consumed by fear. My imagination could spiral into worst-case scenarios faster than I could blink. Anxiety wasn't just a passing feeling. It felt like a shadow that followed me everywhere. If my mind was a battlefield, fear was the atomic bomb that exploded any confidence I'd begun to build.

One memory has always stuck with me: My parents signed me up for an audition with a local youth band. I cried the entire way there, absolutely certain I would humiliate myself. But something shifted when I walked into the room and began to sing. I realized the world didn't end. I didn't fall apart. In fact, I ended up calling my dad afterward, asking if I could stay for the second session. We laugh about it now, but that moment showed me how powerful fear had become in my life and how often it had lied to me.

Even now, fear still tries to creep in. I still get overwhelmed with anxiety about the future, worrying about finances, stepping into a new church, and even writing this book. In those moments, though, I often feel the Lord speak a gentle question into my heart: "After everything I've delivered you from, do you not trust I'll deliver you through this too?" That simple question has the power to stop me in my tracks.

Fear Is Loud, But God's Voice Is Louder

Fear tells us we're not safe, that we're alone, and that the pain will always win. For survivors of abuse, fear often becomes a default mode, not because you're weak or faithless, but because you've learned to protect yourself in environments where you weren't protected. Fear, in that context, isn't just emotional; it's instinctual. It kept you alert, aware, and surviving. But the Lord never meant for you to live in survival mode forever.

God's Word speaks directly into that space. The phrase "Do not fear" appears dozens of times throughout Scripture, and that's just one of the ways God calls His people away from fear. If you include other variations like "fear not" or "do not be afraid," you'll see this reminder *hundreds* of times. That's not a coincidence; that's intentionality. That's a Father who knows how easily fear finds us and how deeply we need His presence to silence it. The key to overcoming fear isn't pushing through it on your own. It's facing it with the name of Jesus on your lips and walking forward knowing that you are already held, even when your knees are shaking.

Fear and Faith Speak Different Languages

Fear is the belief that something bad will happen. Faith is the belief that something good can still come. Fear is rooted in what might go wrong. Faith is anchored in Who is always right. If you've experienced abuse, you've likely heard this lie: "God won't show up this time. He didn't last time. You're on your own."

Let me gently remind you: You are not alone. You were never alone. God is not the author of your abuse. But He is the Author of your healing. The presence of fear doesn't mean you've failed God. It means you're human. It means you've been hurt. But you don't have to live bound to it. Scripture says, *"For the Spirit God gave us does not make us timid, but gives us power, love and self-discipline"* (2 Timothy 1:7). That means you can rebuild safety and peace inside you again, not because trauma didn't happen, but because God is greater than the trauma. His Spirit gives you the strength to walk free.

When Healing Feels Like a Risk

Fear doesn't only live in our minds; it settles in our bodies. It can cause our hearts to race, our breath to shorten, and our muscles to tighten. And when you've walked through trauma, your body remembers. Even after the danger has passed, fear can still grip you unexpectedly.

When I was diagnosed with a health condition called postural orthostatic tachycardia syndrome (POTS), fear hit me hard. Breathing became difficult. Singing, the very thing I felt called to do, suddenly seemed impossible. Doctors told me to avoid deep breaths and standing for long periods, both essential to leading worship. I remember asking God, *Why would You call me to something I can't physically do?*

But God didn't remove the calling. And He didn't remove the fear overnight. Instead, He met me in it. Through professors, doctors, accommodations, and His steady, astounding grace, I began to do what once felt impossible. Not all at once, but through a series of small, painful, and faithful moments. One day of trusting at a time. One song at a time. One breath at a time. It took me enduring a hundred little hard moments, moments of trembling hands, weakness, and uncertainty, before I could stand in the place I'd once been told was impossible for someone with POTS.

Overcoming fear often looks like that. Whether you're facing trauma, illness, or anxiety, the path forward isn't about pretending fear doesn't exist; it's about trusting the One who walks with you through it. During my recovery, I entered a cardiac rehab program. I couldn't run at first, or even walk quickly. But each day, I showed up. Slowly, through repetition and rest, my heart began to strengthen. And I believe that overcoming fear works the same way. Not through one grand act of courage, but through a rhythm of small, consistent steps: journaling a prayer, memorizing a verse, reaching out to someone who can speak truth over you, showing up to worship even when your voice is shaking.

This is how faith grows, not by waiting for fear to disappear, but by learning to trust the faithful God who strengthens you every step of the way. As you grow in that trust, you'll start to notice the patterns fear takes in your life and the moments it tries to steal your peace or your joy. In the next section, we'll explore how to face those moments with wisdom, grace, and truth, holding tightly to the promise that God walks beside you through every trial and trembling heart.

Five Steps to Face Fear with God's Power

Just like physical therapy retrains your body after trauma, overcoming fear retrains your nervous system, your spirit, and your sense of safety. After I was diagnosed with POTS, I had to learn to stand again, walk again, and even breathe differently.

My body wasn't broken; it had simply forgotten what steady ground felt like. That's what fear does too. It doesn't mean your faith is weak. It means your body and soul need gentle retraining. Facing fear isn't about pushing through; it's about healing with God, step by step.

So here are five gentle and trauma-informed steps to face fear with God's power. These are not a checklist to "fix" yourself, but an invitation to walk slowly with Jesus in a way that honors your story and your nervous system. You may return to them again and again, and that is okay. Healing isn't rushed, and every step you take with Him counts.

First, lay your fear at Jesus's feet. Think of it like setting down a heavy backpack you have carried too long. Every time you hand your fear to God, your shoulders breathe a little freer. You were never meant to carry this burden alone. Trauma may have taught you to guard everything tightly, but Jesus invites you to bring your fear, hypervigilance, and grief to Him as often as you need. You don't have to do it once and get it right. You can return to Him again and again.

Next, gently name where fear began. Sometimes fear feels like it comes out of nowhere, but often it is tied to a wound, maybe from someone who should have protected you or from a moment when you were silenced or shamed. Naming the root doesn't mean reliving it. It is simply acknowledging it. If this feels too heavy, let a counselor, therapist, or trauma-informed mentor hold space with you. Think of it like pointing to a scar. You don't have to reopen the wound, but noticing where it formed helps you understand why it still aches.

Third, surround your mind with God's truth. Fear often

echoes the enemy's lies, but Scripture gently reorients us to God's safety and love. Write down verses that remind you of His presence, protection, and care. Place them where you will see them often, not as pressure to memorize or perform faith, but as reminders that you are not unprotected or alone. It is like keeping a candle burning in a dark room. The small, steady light reminds you that the darkness doesn't win.

Fourth, stay close to safe people. Trauma thrives in silence and isolation. Being surrounded by safe people is like sitting beside a campfire. You don't have to touch the flame to feel its warmth. Just being near them brings comfort and steadiness. Healing grows in the presence of trustworthy, steady relationships. Whether it is a counselor, support group, close friend, or mentor, being near safe people helps your nervous system relearn what security feels like. You don't have to share every detail. Sometimes it is enough to simply not be alone.

Finally, notice what is good. Paul wrote in Philippians 4:8 to think on whatever is true, whatever is noble, and whatever is right. This isn't about ignoring pain but gently shifting your focus when anxiety takes over. Maybe it is remembering a moment God came through for you, noticing something beautiful in nature, or simply breathing in God's nearness. Healing also means preparing for the moments when fear sneaks in through triggers. Meeting those moments without shame, and with tools that are both practical and holy, allows you to walk forward in freedom. Think of it like learning to spot wildflowers growing between cracks in the pavement. Beauty can live even in hard places, and it reminds us that God is still here and still at work.

When Triggers Hit: Recognizing Without Shame

For many survivors of trauma and abuse, healing includes learning how to live with triggers and post-traumatic stress disorder (PTSD), those unseen storms that can suddenly rise and threaten to overwhelm us. PTSD is a mental health condition that can develop after we've lived through something deeply distressing or threatening, something that shakes our sense of safety or identity. Earlier in the book, I shared that I was diagnosed with PTSD a few months after the breakup. At the time, I didn't have language for what I was experiencing. I just knew I felt constantly on edge, emotionally flooded, and exhausted from trying to hold it all together. That diagnosis didn't define me, but it helped me begin to understand what was happening inside me and gave me the first steps toward healing.

When most people hear the term PTSD, they think of soldiers returning from war, and that makes sense, because combat trauma is real and significant. But what many don't realize is that PTSD doesn't just happen on battlefields. According to the World Health Organization, approximately 70 percent of people in the world will experience a potentially traumatic event during their lifetime, but only 5.6 percent will go on to develop PTSD.[9] That means there are countless people, just like you and me, learning to navigate life after all kinds of invisible wounds: heartbreak, abuse, betrayal, loss, and fear.

It's important to remember that not everyone who experiences abuse will be diagnosed with PTSD. Trauma shows up differently in every person. Some may carry the weight of anxiety, hypervigilance, or emotional exhaustion without ever receiving a formal diagnosis. Others might find themselves reacting strongly to certain moments or situations, things that seem small on the surface but stir up deep emotional responses. These are called triggers, and they're often unexpected. A sound, a scent, a place, or even a passing comment can suddenly transport you back to a painful memory, flooding your body with fear, panic, or sadness. These moments can feel confusing and disorienting, especially when you can't explain why you're reacting so strongly. But here's what I want you to know: experiencing triggers doesn't mean you're broken. It means you're human. And even in those vulnerable places, God is near.

When a trigger strikes, try to recognize it without shame. Take a deep breath and remind yourself that this feeling, as overwhelming as it may be, is a signal, not a sentence. It's your body saying, "This hurt is still real, and I need care." Naming the experience as a trigger helps remove its power to surprise or shame you. In those moments, anchor yourself in God's presence. Cry out to Him with whatever words you can muster: "Lord, help me," "Jesus, be near," or simply, "You are here." Scripture reminds us that *"The Lord is close to the brokenhearted"* (Psalm 34:18). He is present even in your most fragile moments, holding you steady when your heart races and your mind spins.

One of the most memorable exercises I have ever witnessed for finding peace took place at a camp. We were invited to sit quietly and write down every emotion we were feeling in that very moment: The fear, the loneliness, the anxiety, the heaviness weighing on our hearts. On the opposite side of the page was a list of God's names, each one a tender reminder of who He is and how He meets us exactly where we are.

Then, slowly, we drew lines connecting each emotion to a name of God that felt like a covering, lifeline, or shelter for that feeling. For my fear, I connected to Jehovah-Shalom, "The Lord is peace." This was a gentle reminder that even when my heart raced and my mind spun, God's peace was still holding me. When I felt unseen and alone, I reached for El Roi, "The God who sees," who knows every tear I've shed and every silent cry. When I felt broken beyond repair, I clung to Jehovah-Rapha, "the Lord who heals," and mends every broken heart.

Here are some of the beautiful names we reflected on, each one full of promise and power:

1. **Elohim:** The strong Creator
2. **Yahweh (YHWH):** The personal Lord
3. **Adonai:** Sovereign Master
4. **El Shaddai:** God Almighty, All-Sufficient
5. **El Elyon:** Most High God
6. **Jehovah-Jireh:** The Lord will provide
7. **Jehovah-Rapha:** The Lord who heals
8. **Jehovah-Nissi:** The Lord is my banner, my victory
9. **Jehovah-Shalom:** The Lord is peace
10. **Jehovah-Rohi:** The Lord is my shepherd
11. **Jehovah-Shammah:** The Lord is there
12. **Jehovah-Tsidkenu:** The Lord our righteousness
13. **Jehovah-Sabaoth:** Lord of Hosts
14. **El Olam:** Everlasting God
15. **Jehovah-Mekaddishkem:** The Lord who sanctifies you

This exercise was more than words on a page; it was a sacred act of anchoring my heart in God's unchanging character during the highs and lows of the healing journey. It showed me that my feelings, no matter how overwhelming, do not have the final say. God's names carry power to calm, restore, protect, and remind us that we are deeply known, fully loved, and never alone.

In the past few chapters, we've explored how healing isn't just spiritual, it's physical too. Just as therapy and physical care helped me navigate my journey with POTS, I've learned that in moments of panic or emotional overwhelm, the body often needs care before the soul can respond. Sometimes, we can't just "snap out of it" to pray or do a spiritual exercise. Sometimes, the first step toward God is pressing your feet into the floor and remembering you're still here.

And even there ... especially there, God is with you.

He is present in the quiet rhythm of your breath. He's near in the warmth of a mug in your hands, the weight of a blanket wrapped around your shoulders, the stillness as you place your hand on your chest and remind yourself, *I am safe now*. These aren't just coping tools. They are small, sacred moments when your body catches up with your spirit and where the Spirit of God meets you with gentleness, not pressure.

These physical practices don't replace Scripture or the healing work God does in your soul; they create a doorway to it. God doesn't demand you bypass your body to reach Him. He created it. He knows what it needs. And He is present in every trembling breath, every grounding touch, and every slow return to peace.

When you pair these physical tools with the spiritual act of naming who God is—your Shepherd, your Healer, your Peace, your Everlasting Father—you're building a rhythm of healing that honors both your body and your soul. This is the slow, grace-filled work of restoration. Fear may speak loudly, but you're not standing alone in the fight.

A Final Word to the Wounded

Your fear is valid. Your pain is real. And so is your power in Christ Jesus. The enemy wants to keep you stuck in fear, believing that what happened to you defines your future. But Jesus came to set captives free, not just from sin, but from shame, from fear, and from the lie that you'll never be safe again. Let your fear be a signal, not that God has failed, but that you're being invited to trust Him in a deeper way.

You are loved, and you are held. You don't have to be fearless to move forward; you just have to have enough faith to take the next step. Even if your voice trembles. Even if your knees shake. Even if all you can do is whisper the name of Jesus. That's enough. He'll meet you there.

Your Page to Write: Where Healing Meets Action

1. Bring Your Burdens to Jesus

Take time today to honestly bring your fears to Jesus, whether it's anxiety, hypervigilance, grief, or something else. Write them down or pray about what you're carrying, asking

God to hold it with you.

2. Reflect on Your Story

Think about where fear first took root in your life. Invite God to meet you in that place, trusting He understands your pain and wants to walk with you through it.

3. Saturate Your Mind With Scripture

Choose one verse at a time to meditate on and memorize. Let God's truth fill your mind, especially when fear threatens to overwhelm you.

4. Use Grounding Tools

When panic or overwhelm strikes, try simple physical comforts like holding a warm mug, wrapping yourself in a weighted blanket, or feeling your feet on the ground. These help your body feel safe while your heart leans into God's truth.

5. Stay Connected to Safe People

Surround yourself with God-honoring friends, mentors, or counselors who can walk with you patiently and lovingly as you face your fears.

6. Take Small, Faithful Steps

Each day, focus on what is true rather than what frightens you. Celebrate every small act of trust and courage.

7. Be Gentle With Yourself

Remember, healing from fear is a journey, not a race. God is with you every step of the way, and He's never in a hurry.

SAFE PLACES FOR
SHATTERED HEARTS

"Alone, we can do so little; together we can do so much."
– commonly attributed to Helen Keller

There was a moment in my life that shattered everything I thought I knew about safety, trust, and faith. Right when I had thought I was finally moving forward in my healing journey, it hit me. I had come a long way from the brokenness I once carried, but then I found out something disturbing about someone I was deeply close to. He was one of my main spiritual mentors throughout college and one of the reasons I continued to pursue God's calling on my life when I was ready to give up. The news hit me like a punch to the gut. It rocked me to my core.

Suddenly, everything felt fragile, especially the church. The very place I leaned on for support felt unfamiliar and unsafe. I was flooded with questions, like *How could someone who helped lead me to Jesus hide such darkness? How could my community miss it?* I felt betrayed, isolated, and angry. For a moment, I wanted to walk away altogether.

But then something unexpected happened. People showed up. Tenderly, quietly, and fully. They didn't try to fix my pain with neat answers. They listened. They cried with me. They held space. They prayed when I couldn't. And in that sacred space of being held, I caught a glimpse of the church as God intended it ... not perfect, but present. Not polished, but healing.

This is the power and the complexity of community.

The Gift of Safe Community

All throughout this journey, whether we were talking about identity, therapy, forgiveness, or fear, one thread kept showing up: the importance of having people in your corner. Healing is not something we're meant to navigate on our own. A safe community is essential, not optional. We need people who will speak truth when we forget who we are, sit with us in our sorrow, and gently point us back to Jesus when the weight feels too heavy. That's why this chapter is devoted entirely to the gift of community, because the road to healing, though deeply personal, is never meant to be walked alone.

But let's be honest: The church is not perfect. It's made up of flawed people who sometimes hurt others deeply, even in places meant to be safe. If your abuser was someone from the church, or someone who claimed to follow Jesus, your journey might feel even more complicated. Betrayal and broken trust from within faith communities can make the idea of belonging again feel terrifying. But acknowledging the wounds doesn't mean rejecting the healing God can still bring through others. The solution isn't to shut the door on community entirely. It's to seek out spaces that prioritize safety, healing, and truth. And it's okay to find new places that aren't tied to what hurt you. God's love isn't limited to one building or one group. He will meet you where healing is possible.

Community is essential because it breaks the isolation that wounds often create. Pain kept hidden grows heavier. But when we share it with others who understand, the burden lightens.

Community reminds us we are not defined by our hurt but by the love that surrounds us. That love becomes a medicine for our souls. Beyond compassion, community offers the kind of encouragement that fuels us when despair creeps in. It reminds us of our worth and God's promises when we can't see them ourselves. It also brings accountability, not condemnation and shame, but a loving nudge toward growth and freedom.

When the church lives out its calling, it becomes this kind of community ... not perfect, but committed. A family of wounded people walking in grace, supporting and restoring one another. Healing happens here because we're not meant to do this alone. We are held and strengthened by others who help carry the load.

Finding this kind of community takes courage. It may mean seeking out small groups where vulnerability is welcome. It might look like walking with a mentor, joining a healing-focused ministry, or connecting with friends who consistently show up. No group is perfect, but the right one can be a lifeline where hope grows and healing begins.

But community isn't only about receiving. It's also about giving. Healing deepens when we extend grace and support to others. Sharing our stories creates space for mutual healing and builds resilience in the body of Christ.

Sharing Your Story and Becoming a Healing Presence

For a long time, I was afraid to share my story. It felt vulnerable, risky, and real. I feared judgment, rejection, or stirring up old wounds. But eventually, I learned that even in pain, my story held power, not just for me, but for others.

The first time I opened up was at a summer camp where I was leading worship. A young girl approached me after a session. Her burden was heavy — abuse from a parental figure. As she spoke, I recognized the familiar ache of confusion, fear, and isolation. And in that moment, God used my story as a lifeline. She saw she wasn't alone, and she saw hope.

With help from church staff and the right authorities, she began her journey toward safety and healing. That experience transformed me. It showed me the value of community and the beauty of vulnerability. Being known in our brokenness makes space for healing for both ourselves and others.

Since then, I've become more aware of those who are hurting. I can better recognize when someone is in pain and walk alongside them in support. It's not always easy, but it reminds me how interconnected our healing journeys are. The church isn't just where we receive healing, it's where we extend it.

Your story has power too. But there's no pressure or timeline. Healing isn't linear. Vulnerability takes time. Give yourself grace. Be patient. Just because you're not ready to speak doesn't mean your story isn't valuable. But when that tug comes, when God places someone in your path, don't be afraid to answer. You may be surprised how your pain brings someone else peace. And in the sharing, your healing may deepen, too.

Healing is sacred work, but never solitary work. You weren't made to carry your pain alone. God surrounds us with people, imperfect but compassionate, who reflect His love and truth when we forget. The road may still be hard, but you don't have to walk it alone. Let others speak life where you feel most broken. Let their prayers carry you. And one day, you'll be that voice for someone else.

Because healing doesn't just restore. It connects, transforms, and reminds us that even in the deepest pain, we are never truly alone.

As we step into the rest of this book, you'll find that community will remain a vital part of the healing process, whether you're learning to see yourself as beloved, confronting past lies with truth, or setting new boundaries that protect your heart. You weren't made to turn the page in isolation. You were made to turn it surrounded by grace, held by others, and carried by the love of God.

Your Page to Write: Where Healing Meets Action

1. Identify or Seek Out a Safe Community

Take time to think about or find a safe, supportive group where you can eventually share your story. This could be a church small group, a counseling group, or a trusted circle of friends who offer empathy, encouragement, and accountability.

2. Reflect on Your Support System

Consider who in your life, your church, or your wider community might be able to walk alongside you in your healing journey. Who listens well? Who encourages growth? Who offers wise and loving support?

3. Reach Out When You're Ready

When you feel ready, reach out to those trusted people or join a group focused on restoration and healing. It's okay to take this step slowly and on your own timeline. Healing happens best in community. Don't hesitate to invite trusted people into your journey, allowing their presence to lighten your load.

4. Offer Support to Others

As you continue to heal, be open to offering that same support and encouragement to others who are walking through their own struggles. Connection is a two-way street, and mutual care can be deeply healing.

THE SACRED WORK OF HEALING

"We can all see God in exceptional things, but it requires the culture of spiritual discipline to see God in every detail." [10] *— Oswald Chambers*

There was a night I sat in my car, hands gripping the steering wheel, tears blurring my vision, and all I could whisper was, "God, I don't know how to come back from this." I had already been to counseling. I had read the books. I had named the pain. But somehow, healing still felt far away. That night, I didn't need more noise or advice. I needed a way to breathe again and a way to remember I wasn't alone in this. And slowly, gently, that's what the spiritual disciplines became for me. Not rigid religious boxes to check off, but sacred rhythms that brought me back to the heart of God when everything felt like too much. These practices of prayer, Scripture, worship, silence, and journaling became a lifeline. A place to rest. A place to rebuild. They didn't erase the pain, but they anchored me in the Presence that could carry it.

I've said it before, and I'll say it again: Healing takes time. It takes courage. And it takes intention. After deep wounds, especially those caused by people or places that were meant to be safe, our souls often feel lost. We question what's true, who we can trust, and whether we'll ever feel whole again. The journey is complex, filled with therapy appointments, hard conversations, spiritual battles, and quiet moments we don't always know how to name. But through it all, there's one invitation God keeps offering us: Come close. Draw near to Me.

Spiritual disciplines are not a performance. They're not about proving we're strong or holy. They're about returning. They are practices that plant us in the presence of God again and again, until we remember what trauma tried to make us forget. They help us recall the truth that we are loved, safe, seen, and held. These holy habits make space in our lives for God to restore what has been broken. They aren't magic formulas, but they are powerful rhythms that shape our posture toward the Healer. They teach us how to rest, how to reset, how to listen, and how to breathe again. Let's walk through them together.

Reading and Engaging with Scripture

Not just reading, but truly digesting God's Word gives our hearts the nourishment they need to recover. Scripture becomes our anchor when the waves crash in. When shame whispers lies, we remember, *"There is now no condemnation for those who are in Christ Jesus"* (Romans 8:1). When we feel too weak to go on, we return to, *"My grace is sufficient for you, for My power is made perfect in weakness"* (2 Corinthians 12:9). Engaging with Scripture isn't about checking off chapters, it's about meeting God in your hurt.

So how do you truly digest Scripture? Start where your heart is. Pause on the verses that speak to your pain or your hope, and let the words sink in slowly. Eliminate distractions. Ask honest questions. Journal what stirs your soul and invite the Holy Spirit to help you see with fresh eyes. Healing comes not just through knowing Scripture but through letting it settle deep into your heart, where truth can rewrite the lies. It isn't about how much you read; it's about how deeply you let it take root. Let it wash over the places that feel raw. Let it correct, comfort, and call you back to truth. If your mind starts to wander, let it. See where it takes you and use the pages in front of you to respond. In a world that's always shouting lies, Scripture becomes your steady whisper of hope. And in your healing journey, it's not just a guide, it's what holds it all together.

Prayer

I used to think prayer was about saying the right words to get the right results. But over time, through questions I couldn't answer and pain I couldn't fix, I learned that prayer is more about presence than performance.

Someone once asked me, "Why pray if God already knows everything?" And the answer I've come to believe is this: Prayer isn't about changing God's mind. It's about letting God change our hearts and trusting Him to respond in His way and timing. It's an invitation to a relationship. Revelation 3:20 says Jesus stands at the door and knocks, and prayer is how we open it. You don't need fancy words or a perfect formula. Prayer can be spoken out loud, whispered in tears, or written in a journal. It can be a cry for help, a moment of stillness, or a whispered "thank You." Begin with honesty and by thanking God. Tell Him how you really feel and ask for what you need. Then, listen.

Even Jesus, in the Garden of Gethsemane, prayed, *"Not My will, but Yours"* (Matthew 26:39). That's what prayer does. It helps us surrender, trust, and align with God's heart. Prayer is not just a lifeline; it's the steady heartbeat of healing. Let it be your safe place, your daily breath, and your honest connection with the God who's always listening.

Worship

We touched on this briefly before, but worship deserves its own focus in the disciplines because of how deeply it shapes our healing journey. Sometimes, life feels like being lost on a deserted road, isolated, afraid, and unsure. That's the wilderness David faced while hiding in a cave, hunted and alone. Yet even there, he chose worship over panic. In Psalm 57, David exalts God while honestly admitting his weariness and fear. It's in this tension of being honest about pain while still choosing to worship that true healing begins.

Worship isn't about perfect moments or feelings; it's about anchoring our hearts in God's unchanging goodness despite confusion or fear. David's worship was an act of surrender. He praised God amidst enemies and doubt, trusting Him to turn his wilderness into holy ground. Worship isn't just singing or attending church. It's any act or attitude that lifts God above our circumstances and aligns our hearts with His truth. It can be loud praise, silent rest, prayer, going on a walk, making art, playing music, acts of service, or simply focusing on who God is, rather than what's wrong. Worship is meant to reflect God's goodness back to Him.

Journaling

Journaling is a powerful spiritual discipline that helps us process our thoughts, emotions, and experiences as we walk through healing. It's more than just writing down what happened in a day. It is a sacred practice of reflecting on God's work in our lives, recording prayers, and exploring our hearts honestly. Through journaling, we create space to pour out our fears, doubts, gratitude, and hopes, allowing God to meet us in the raw and real places of our journey.

To journal effectively, start by finding a quiet moment where you can be uninterrupted and open. You don't need fancy tools. A simple notebook or even a digital document works fine. Begin by writing whatever is on your mind or heart, without worrying about grammar or structure. You might jot down a prayer, a Scripture that spoke to you, or reflections on how you're feeling that day. Sometimes, asking yourself questions like *What is God teaching me right now?* or *Where do I need His healing today?* can help guide your writing.

Journaling invites honesty. It's okay to write down anger, confusion, or pain. God welcomes all of it. Over time, your journal becomes a record of your growth, a reminder of God's faithfulness, and a tool to clarify your thoughts and emotions. By regularly engaging in this practice, you create a sacred rhythm that opens your heart to deeper healing and greater intimacy with God.

Silence and Solitude

After abuse or trauma, noise can become our coping mechanism. We tend to fill every moment to keep from feeling too much. But silence is where we learn to hear again. Solitude isn't loneliness; it's a sacred space where God meets us in the stillness and reminds us that we're not alone. Solitude invites us to be still, to slow down, and to be fully present with God, allowing His peace to wash over the chaos inside us.

However, for those of us healing from trauma or living with PTSD, solitude and silence can sometimes be challenging or even triggering. When left alone with our thoughts, painful memories, fears, or anxiety can surface unexpectedly, leading to feelings of overwhelm, isolation, or panic. In these moments, solitude can feel less like a sacred refuge and more like a downward spiral of chaos and loneliness. Because of this, it's important to approach silence and solitude with care and intention. If you're new to this discipline or if solitude stirs up difficult emotions, consider starting small: just a few minutes of quiet time each day, and gradually build as you feel safe. It can also help to have a plan in place for when difficult feelings arise, such as journaling your thoughts afterward, praying for peace, or reaching out to a trusted friend or counselor.

Remember, solitude isn't about isolating yourself from support or avoiding community; it's about creating space to deepen your relationship with God. When practiced wisely, silence and solitude can become powerful tools that calm the mind, center the heart, and renew your spirit, giving you the strength to face the healing journey ahead.

Fasting

Fasting is a spiritual practice in which we intentionally give up something, often food, to focus more deeply on God. It's not about punishment or earning favor, but about creating space to prioritize God's presence and rely on Him above all else. Fasting helps us become more aware of God's voice and guidance.

There are many ways to fast, from giving up meals to stepping away from distractions like social media. What matters most is the intention behind it, not the length or strictness. Spiritually, fasting often goes hand-in-hand with prayer and meditation, creating a powerful combination that sharpens our focus on God's will and strengthens our reliance on Him. It can bring clarity in times of decision, humility in times of pride, and strength in times of weakness. Jesus, Himself, fasted before beginning His public ministry, showing us how fasting prepares us for spiritual breakthroughs and deeper encounters with God.

However, fasting should always be done with wisdom and care, especially for those with health issues or a history of trauma. It's not about legalism or self-harm but about drawing nearer to God with a healthy and humble heart.

Ultimately, fasting is a way to say, "God, You are my ultimate source. I'm choosing to depend on You above all else." It's a powerful tool in the healing journey, helping us recalibrate our hearts, break unhealthy attachments, and open ourselves to the redemptive work God wants to do within us.

Serving

Sometimes, healing feels selfish. We get so focused on our own wounds that we wonder if we'll ever have anything to give again. But I've found that serving others, even in small ways, has often unlocked deeper layers of my own healing. Not because it distracts me from my pain, but because it shows me how God can use it. When we serve, we declare that we are not defined by what we've lost; we are participants in what God is still doing.

Serving is about showing God's love through actions that meet the needs of others. It's a way to live out our faith by giving time, energy, and compassion to those around us. Serving isn't just about big gestures. It can be small acts of kindness, listening well, or helping someone in practical ways. When we serve, we step outside ourselves and reflect God's heart for the hurting and vulnerable. Serving connects us to the community and reminds us that healing often happens through relationships and shared burdens. It shifts our focus from our own pain to the needs of others, which can bring a fresh perspective and purpose. Serving is a powerful spiritual discipline that nurtures both the giver and receiver, helping us grow in love, humility, and healing.

Evangelism

Sharing our faith, even from our places of struggle, is a powerful reminder that healing is possible. You don't have to have it all figured out to point someone to Jesus. Sometimes, your story of survival is the very bridge someone else needs to begin their journey. *"We overcome by the blood of the Lamb and the word of our testimony"* (Revelation 12:11). Evangelism is sharing the hope and love of Jesus with others. It's about living out and speaking your faith in ways that invite people to know God's grace and truth. Evangelism isn't just about preaching; it can be simple conversations, acts of kindness, or showing Christ's love through your life.

When we share our faith, we participate in God's work of healing and restoration in the world. Evangelism reminds us that our healing journey isn't just for us. It's also about helping others find freedom and hope. It encourages us to be bold and compassionate, trusting God to work through our words and actions. Evangelism is a spiritual discipline that strengthens our faith and deepens our connection to God's mission, inviting healing for both us and those we reach.

Each of these disciplines is a doorway to healing. Some days, you may step through with confidence. Other days, you may feel like you're crawling. That's okay. These practices are not the goal; they're the pathway. And as we engage with them slowly, intentionally, and imperfectly, we begin to notice something: healing isn't just about feeling better. It's about being transformed.

You may not always feel God moving. But with every whispered prayer, every silent moment of surrender, every verse you cling to in the dark, He is. Healing is rarely instant. But it is happening. So, as you walk through the next chapters, whether they challenge you, comfort you, or call you into deeper surrender, come back to these rhythms. Let them ground you. Let them grow you. Let them remind you that you are never healing alone. Because healing doesn't come through discipline alone. It comes through the presence of a loving God. And these are the practices that help us find Him, again and again.

Your Page to Write: Where Healing Meets Action

1. Choose One Practice to Begin

Select one spiritual discipline to focus on this week. This might be spending a few minutes daily reading and reflecting on Scripture, praying with honesty and openness, journaling your thoughts and emotions, or carving out a moment of intentional silence and solitude.

2. Approach With Gentleness

Remember, there is no "right" way to practice or perfect outcome to achieve. Be gentle with yourself as you explore this new rhythm.

3. Take Small, Steady Steps

Let this practice be a simple, consistent way to reconnect with God's presence and create an anchor for your healing journey.

4. Notice the Impact on Your Heart

Pay attention to how this discipline shifts your heart and mind, even if the changes are small at first.

5. Return Regularly

Keep returning to this practice as a lifeline, especially during times when pain feels overwhelming or healing feels distant.

FIXING OUR EYES FORWARD

"Forget the former things; do not dwell on the past. See, I am doing a new thing! Now it springs up; do you not perceive it? I am making a way in the wilderness and streams in the wasteland." – Isaiah 43:18-19

I struggle to walk in a straight line. It sounds odd, but it's true. Wherever my eyes wander, my body tends to follow. If I look left, I drift left. If I look right, I drift right. This often causes me to bump into things, and my husband frequently pokes fun at me because I accidentally veer into him while we walk side by side. It's a silly struggle, but it vividly illustrates a deeper truth: We tend to go wherever our focus leads us.

The same principle applies to our healing journey and emotional well-being. In Matthew 6:22-23, Jesus says, *"The eye is the lamp of the body. If your eyes are healthy, your whole body will be full of light. But if your eyes are unhealthy, your whole body will be full of darkness. If then the light within you is darkness, how great is that darkness!"* When we fix our eyes on God, He leads us on a path of healing, growth, and hope. But when our attention stays locked on the past, on pain, regret, fear, or failure, we can drift into patterns that trap us in cycles of sorrow and immobility. The past has a place in our story, but it does not define our destination. In Christ, our future is full of promise.

Even after we've been delivered from something painful, we often live as if we're still stuck in it. When I was diagnosed with PTSD, I finally had clarity, but I also found a false identity in the diagnosis. I lived with one foot in my trauma and the other in the present. And for a while, I accepted that restricted space. PTSD causes people to relive trauma repeatedly, and I unknowingly allowed that experience to justify staying in survival mode. Instead of stepping into healing, I lived in the shadow of my past, rather than under the refuge of the Almighty's wings.

But God's plan was never for us to remain prisoners of our history. If it were, Jesus's death and resurrection would have no purpose. His healing and restoration would be out of reach. But the truth is: because of Christ, you are not stuck. And you are not alone.

When the Past Becomes a Prison

Many people, even those without PTSD, live as if their past still owns them. They don't fully embrace the freedom Christ has given. They carry shame, brokenness, and pain like permanent baggage, forgetting that God is always working to restore what's been lost.

Consider the story of Lot's family in Genesis 19. When two angels warned them to flee Sodom before its destruction, they were instructed not to look behind them. But Lot's wife did. And in that moment of disobedience, she was turned into a pillar of salt, literally frozen in place. Her longing for what was behind her cost her the chance to move forward.

When we cling to our past, our wounds, regrets, or familiar dysfunction, we can become just as stuck. We risk missing out on the future God is preparing, simply because we can't take our eyes off what we've left behind. But forward movement requires a forward focus. Fix your gaze on Jesus, not the ruins He rescued you from. When we linger on the past, we lose spiritual momentum and fall back into old patterns that no longer serve us. We drain our energy on memories that He's already redeemed.

Freedom in Forward Focus

This doesn't mean we just "get over" trauma or bypass the pain. Healing is holy work. It takes time, surrender, and daily choices to partner with God in the restoration process. You release the past piece by piece, day by day. And God meets you in the process, making all things new.

Jesus didn't stay on the cross. He endured the suffering, but His eyes were on the joy of redemption set before Him. Likewise, God has already resurrected you from your past, so why keep returning to the graveyard? The enemy wants to drag you back. He'll remind you of everything you did wrong and every reason why you're not enough. But Satan has no future, only a past to throw in your face. Jesus, on the other hand, has forgiven you and given you a new identity. Psalm 103:12 says, *"As far as the east is from the west, so far has He removed our transgressions from us."*

When you surrender your past to Jesus, He doesn't just cover it; He reclaims it for His glory. And the pain that once defined you becomes part of your testimony of victory. The trials you've faced don't disqualify you; they prepare you. But if you choose to live in the past, you'll miss the future God has for you. Bitterness, shame, and blame keep us bound. But Jesus came to set us free. So, you get to choose: will you be a prisoner of what was, or a participant in what God is doing now?

Your Page to Write: Where Healing Meets Action

1. Make the Decision to Move Forward

If you've been walking through a season of healing, decide today to keep pressing onward. Choose to shift your focus away from what hurt you and toward what God is doing in your life.

2. Practice Daily Surrender

Each day, intentionally surrender your past through prayer, journaling, or quiet reflection. Remind yourself that healing isn't a single event, but a faithful process God promises to complete (Philippians 1:6).

3. Resist Being Pulled Backward

Don't let the enemy drag you backward into pain or doubt. Remember, the One who holds your future is stronger than anything behind you.

4. Step Into the Next Chapter

As you move forward, navigating new relationships, setting healthy boundaries, and learning to trust again, hold tightly to this truth: you were made for more than survival.

5. Embrace Your Purpose to Thrive

You were created not just to endure, but to thrive in God's grace and hope.

PART THREE

The Pages That

Speak Courage

LEARNING LOVE FROM THE ONE WHO MADE IT

"But the kind of love that God created and demonstrated is a costly one because it involves sacrifice and presence. It's a love that operates more like a sign language than being spoken outright." [11] *—Bob Goff*

After everything fell apart, I remember sitting on the floor, with mascara running down my cheeks, half laughing, half crying with my closest friends. I kept saying, "I'm never dating again. I'll get a bunch of dogs, maybe a houseplant, and call it a day." And I meant it. My heart felt like it had been chewed up and spit out. Love? That word felt like a cruel joke. The thought of trusting someone again, of letting someone close enough to hurt me, felt not just risky, but impossible.

But somewhere deep in me, beyond the hurt, there was this whisper: *What if love could look different? What if healing didn't mean closing the door forever, but learning to open it slowly, carefully, and with wisdom and God's guidance?*

Healing from an abusive relationship is one of the hardest journeys anyone can face. Imagine standing on the shore, wounded and vulnerable, staring out at a vast ocean where dangerous creatures might be lurking beneath the surface. It feels terrifying to even consider stepping into those waters again. You might wonder, *Why would I ever risk putting myself out there when the danger is so real?* After experiencing deep pain, the thought of opening your heart again can feel impossible, like jumping into that ocean, knowing you could be hurt or broken all over again.

Abuse twists everything we thought we knew about love and about ourselves. It's like the ground has shifted beneath us without warning. You begin to question everything—your worth, your decisions, your ability to set boundaries. Trust becomes foreign, and every step forward feels like a risk. If you're reading this and feel that confusion or ache, I want you to hear this: *Love itself did not hurt you. A person who didn't know how to love did.* We weren't made to live alone. From the beginning, God designed us for connection. This is why He created Eve for Adam, because longing for love is natural and good. But when your heart longs for love while your soul trembles with fear, what do you do? How do you take that next step without falling again?

There Is No Fear in Love

The Bible offers powerful encouragement for those of us wrestling with fear after abuse. 1 John 4:18 says, *"There is no fear in love (dread does not exist). But perfect love drives out fear ..."* Fear, especially the kind that lingers after trauma, is often tied to the expectation of pain. But God's perfect love casts out that fear.

God is not only the Creator of love, He is love. In 1 John 4:16, John tells us, *"God is love."* Just as ice cannot be anything but cold, God cannot be anything but love. His love is eternal, unfailing, and pure. It's that kind of love that led Him to send Jesus to carry our brokenness and sin on the cross. So if you're wondering whether real love could've been the thing that hurt you, hear this again: God's perfect love never wounds or betrays. What hurt you was someone who did not reflect or live by that love. God's love drives out fear, doubt, and insecurity. And every time you catch a glimpse of real love in this world, you're catching a glimpse of His heart for you. If you choose to step back into relationships, hold on to this truth: Fear doesn't exist in perfect love. Let God's love be your safe place as you heal and hope again.

Why Date?

If you're reading this, chances are you've experienced some kind of relationship violence. And maybe you're asking, *Why would I want to date again after what I went through?* That is a valid and important question, one only you can answer.

Now I'm not here to say whether you should or shouldn't date. That's a personal decision. Some people find peace in singleness; others long for companionship but are scared of being hurt again. Wherever you land, I want to bring you back to the purpose of dating.

Dating is a process of discernment. It's not about chasing someone to fix your loneliness or complete you. It's about prayerfully discovering whether someone aligns with God's plan for your life. It's not a race or a checklist; it's an opportunity to build something meaningful and with intentionality. You are already whole and already deeply loved by God. You are not half a person waiting to be completed. You are not broken beyond repair. The only thing we ever truly lack is more of God's love and nearness, which fills every void. I once heard a quote that stuck with me. It said, "Your friends, family, or significant other are not the source of your fulfillment. They are resources. God is your source."

So if you choose to date, seek someone who strengthens your

faith and mirrors God's love. And remember, not every relationship will lead to marriage, and that's okay. Each experience teaches, refines, and prepares us for what's ahead.

Redefining Relationships

As you re-enter the world of relationships, it's important to examine how you view them. It's easy to fall into a consumer mindset and treat dating like shopping for the best deal: looks, charm, wealth, etc. But love isn't a product to consume. It's a partnership built on mutual respect, shared values, and a desire to glorify God together.

Instead of looking for the "perfect person," look for a companion. Someone with genuine character, steady faith, and a heart anchored in God. Relationships grow through time, not instant chemistry. First impressions can be deceiving. I learned this the hard way. The person I thought I loved turned out to be very different beneath the surface. And truth be told, if I had been walking closely with God during that season, I may have seen the red flags earlier.

The Bible gives us a guide for what true love looks like. The kind of love God extends toward us is called agape love, and it is the highest, most selfless form. It's the kind of love that sacrifices, stays, and doesn't fail. Jesus displayed agape love through His life and death. And Paul describes this love in 1 Corinthians 13, which can serve as a roadmap for how we should both give and receive love.

Understanding this list is more than just memorizing it. It's about setting standards so that you can recognize when they are, or aren't, being met. It will protect your heart and keep your relationships aligned with God's original design.

The Definition of True Agape Love (1 Corinthians 13:4-8)

Love is patient.

Love is kind.

Love does not envy.

Love does not boast.

Love is not proud.

Love does not dishonor others.

Love is not self-seeking.

Love is not easily angered.

Love does not delight in evil but rejoices in truth.

Love always protects.

Love always trusts.

Love always hopes.

Love always perseveres.

Love never fails.

Love Is Safe: Patient, Kind, Not Easily Angered, Always Protects

Real love isn't in a hurry, and it doesn't play games. It gives you room to grow, mess up, and still be fully seen and accepted. Patience says, "I'm not here for the polished version of you. I'm here for *you*, right now, even in the messy middle." Kindness, the real kind, isn't given as bait or a bargaining chip. It doesn't say, "I'll be good to you *if*..." It's steady and safe. And when love is safe, it won't explode in anger when things get tough. Instead, it steps in and shields you physically, emotionally, and spiritually. It gives you space to breathe again.

After some time had passed, I started dipping my toe back into the dating world. I met a guy who, on paper, seemed great. He said the right things, acted the right way, but every time I was around him, I felt this rising wave of anxiety I couldn't explain. It was like my body knew something my brain hadn't caught up to yet. That's when I realized, after walking through abuse, my sensitivity had changed. My heart had been trained to notice when something felt off.

But here's an important distinction. Sometimes, what we call "gut feelings" are really the effects of unresolved trauma—hypervigilance that keeps us on edge, even when we're safe. Other times, that unsettled feeling is the Holy Spirit giving us discernment. One way to sort through the difference is to hold those gut reactions up to what God says about love. Does this relationship reflect the patience, kindness, safety, and truth that Scripture describes? Or does it stir up confusion, fear, or shame? God's voice will always align with His Word and His character, and His love never leaves you anxious or unsafe.

So listen to your body, but don't stop there. Bring those feelings before God, compare them with what His Word says, and invite trusted people to walk with you. When you stay close to Him, He'll help you see what's true before you get too deep to escape. Real discernment leads to peace. Real love won't keep you on edge; it will keep you safe.

Love Is Humble: Not Proud, Not Boastful, Not Self-Seeking

There's no room for ego in a healthy relationship. Love doesn't need to be the loudest in the room or the one who always wins. A humble partner doesn't need to be right all the time. They're willing to apologize, to listen, and to learn. They don't see you as a project that needs fixing; they see you as a partner.

When I was with my abuser, I remember how every

disagreement turned into a competition. I felt small whenever I had a different opinion. But love rooted in humility doesn't make you feel like you're walking on eggshells. It invites honesty, even when it's uncomfortable. Humility says, "Your heart matters more than being right." It listens. It apologizes first. It doesn't see vulnerability as weakness but as a bridge to a deeper connection. When you think about the kind of love you want, don't just look for someone kind or charming. Look for someone willing to grow, to admit when they've messed up, and to lead with grace over pride.

Love Is Secure: It Does Not Envy, Always Trusts, Rejoices in Truth

Love doesn't keep you on a short leash. It celebrates your individuality. There's no jealousy, no games. Instead, there's trust that is open-handed, steady, and built on truth. It doesn't manipulate or gaslight. Secure love is rooted in honesty and mutual confidence.

In my past relationship, I often felt like I was treated as someone's possession rather than a partner. My abuser never trusted me. Every text, every conversation, and every moment was met with suspicion and control. That kind of love breeds jealousy, doubt, and fear. It's exhausting and damaging because it steals away your sense of safety and worth.

Trust is the foundation of any real relationship, but once you've been betrayed, learning to trust again can feel impossible. It's a vulnerable and slow process. You question your own judgment and wonder if you'll ever be safe enough to fully open your heart. But God's love teaches us a different way, a love that trusts deeply, that does not envy or control, but celebrates truth and transparency. Secure love frees you from the prison of suspicion and invites you into a space where you are known, respected, and honored for exactly who you are. It's not easy to get there, but with God's help, trust can be rebuilt and love can feel safe again.

Love Is Resilient: Always Hopes, Always Perseveres, Never Fails

After everything I went through, believing that love could last felt nearly impossible. When abuse shatters your heart, it seems like love is fragile, easily broken, and maybe even out of reach. But resilient love, the kind God calls us to, doesn't give up. It keeps hoping and keeps persevering through pain, doubts, and setbacks.

My own story of resilient love didn't come easily. My husband and I were in a long-distance relationship for three years before we got married. That kind of distance tests your commitment every day. We had to actively choose love, not just once, but every single day and in every single moment. We pushed through the hard moments, the loneliness, and the uncertainties to reach the blessing of marriage. It wasn't perfect, and it wasn't always easy, but we made a commitment to fight for each other when things got tough.

I am so blessed that the man I married exemplified that perseverance and steadfast love. Together, we chose to hope and believe in the possibility of joy and unity, even when the path was difficult. That choice to persevere, through every trial, is what brought us to a love that is stronger, deeper, and truly resilient.

And through it all, I've come to see that this resilience mirrors the very nature of God's love for us. God's love never fails, never gives up, and never runs out of hope, even when we stumble, doubt, or feel unworthy. His love perseveres through every hard season, calling us to trust that no matter how difficult the journey, His love is the steady foundation that never breaks. When we anchor ourselves in that perfect love, we too can learn to hope, to persevere, and to love with a resilience that reflects the heart of God.

Healing after abuse isn't about rushing into love again; it's about learning what love truly is and allowing God to reshape your view of it. It's about rebuilding trust slowly, setting new standards, and letting His truth replace old lies. You are not the same person who once accepted less than you deserved. You are stronger now, wiser, and grounded in the knowledge that you are deeply loved by a God whose love never fails. So, if someone comes into your life, let them meet this version of you, the one who knows what love is and isn't. The one who has been held and healed by God. And if no one else walks in just yet, know that you are already walking in the greatest love there is.

Let agape love be your filter, not your fear. Use it to set your standards because if you never list what your standards are, you'll never know when they aren't being met. Let it guide you toward relationships that reflect the heart of Christ. You're not starting over. You're simply preparing for what lies ahead, with eyes wide open, and a heart fully seen.

Your Page to Write: Where Healing Meets Action

1. Reflect on Your Fears

Take a quiet moment to consider any fears you still carry about love and relationships. Write them down honestly.

2. Bring God's Word to Your Fears

Next to each fear, write what God says about love in Scripture, especially from 1 John 4:18 (*"There is no fear in love..."*) and 1 Corinthians 13. Let these truths gently replace your fears.

3. Define Your Relationship Standards

Create a list of qualities you want to see in a future partner, grounded in how God defines love. Use 1 Corinthians 13 as your guide: patience, kindness, humility, trustworthiness, perseverance, and more. Be as specific as you can.

4. Keep Your List as a Reminder

Let this list be a steady reminder of the kind of love you were made for, a love rooted in God's perfect example.

5. Approach Future Relationships Intentionally

If or when you begin dating again, do so with intention. Let God lead your steps, and let His agape love be your guiding light in every choice you make.

YOU WEREN'T MADE TO SETTLE

"Do not be yoked together with unbelievers. For what do righteousness and wickedness have in common? Or what fellowship can light have with darkness?" — 2 Corinthians 6:14

The story of my husband and me didn't begin with fireworks or some big, cinematic moment. It began with a quiet conversation. We met at a Christian camp, where he played drums, and I was a vocalist on the worship team. One evening, early on, we found ourselves sitting across from each other in a cabin, talking long after rehearsal ended. We asked questions, some lighthearted, some deep, and some intentionally hard. Beneath it all, we were both trying to discover the same thing: Is Jesus truly the center of this person's life?

We weren't interested in just finding someone who believed in God. We had both been through relationships where belief wasn't matched by intimacy with Jesus, and we'd felt the heartbreak that comes from being unequally yoked. So we didn't avoid the real questions. We weren't looking for someone to check boxes. We were looking for someone whose life reflected a surrendered walk with Christ.

That night, I had no idea the man across from me would one day become my husband. But even then, I could sense something sacred unfolding. It was something built not on chemistry alone, but on a shared desire to follow Jesus. And that became the foundation we would keep building on, one faithful step at a time.

Starting with Christ, Not Adding Him Later

There's something profoundly different about a relationship that starts with Christ at its center. That foundation made all the difference for us. But unfortunately, many people wait too long to ask the important spiritual questions. They wait until they've already become emotionally entangled, until the feelings are strong, the memories are made, and the connection is deep. Only then do they try to wedge Jesus into the picture, hoping He'll somehow bless a relationship that didn't start with Him.

Ladies, you are called to be a wife, not a babysitter. Similarly, men are called to be leaders, not settlers. If someone doesn't know Jesus intimately, it is not your job to carry the weight of their salvation while also trying to build a life together. That is a burden only Christ Himself can carry.

I've seen time and again what happens when people don't understand what love from God really is. They chase counterfeit versions, such as love rooted in lust, loneliness, or emotional convenience. And every time the enemy offers fake love, it's an attempt to distract us from the real thing. When your heart is chasing false intimacy, it's no longer chasing God.

Take King Solomon, for example. In 1 Kings 11, Solomon knew God's commands. He was told not to marry foreign women because they would turn his heart toward other gods, and that's exactly what happened. Scripture says Solomon "loved many foreign women," and that decision drew him away from the Lord. He didn't lack wisdom. He lacked obedience. And just like Solomon, we, too, can find ourselves ignoring God's voice because we're determined to have what we want, even if it costs us God's best.

God gives warnings for a reason. He doesn't use them to restrict us, but to protect us. Just as a parent guides and sets boundaries for their children out of love, God sets boundaries for our hearts. If we ignore His guidance and give ourselves away too easily, we risk becoming entangled in relationships built on the world's standards, not His. But even when we've gone down that path, there's still hope. Because God's love can set you free. It can heal the places where counterfeit love broke you.

Learning to Recognize What's Real

Romans 1:24–27 reminds us of what happens when we exchange truth for a lie. When we allow culture, feelings, or lust to define love, we miss out on God's truth. Worse, we begin to worship a version of God that doesn't exist—one that changes with our emotions and comfortable with sin. But that's not the God of the Bible.

Let me give you a picture that helped me understand this more clearly. During spring break one year, I was thrifting with my mom and came across a designer-looking bag in a bin. It was marked $15. Inside, it was labeled "Louis Vuitton." I didn't know right away if it was authentic, so I began to research and inspect it. Turns out, it was real. I had unknowingly picked up a $2,000 handbag for just $15. The person who gave it away clearly didn't know what they had.

God's love is like that. If we don't know what real love looks like, if we're not familiar with it, then we'll never recognize its worth. We'll settle for the fake because it looks shiny on the outside. Or worse, we'll walk away from something real because we don't recognize its value.

That's why discernment matters so much in relationships. You want to be with someone who will fight with you, not against you. Someone who will pray with you, stand beside you in spiritual battles, and call out the lies of the enemy over your life. A partner who walks in truth and pushes you closer to Christ, not further away.

All the time, I hear people say, "That kind of love doesn't exist anymore," and I used to wonder if they were right. My husband once believed he'd never get married. After years of heartbreak and hollow connections, he couldn't imagine anything different. I felt the same. Love had started to feel like a risk not worth taking.

But before we ever crossed paths, God was doing something in both of us. Quietly and faithfully, He was leading us out of shallow relationships and back to Himself. There came a point where we each had to let go of timelines, of expectations, of the desire to be chosen, and lay our desires at His feet. Not as a bargaining chip, but as an act of surrender. Then, we had to trust that if He wanted to bring someone into our lives, He would. We had to give up control and stop trying to manufacture a relationship ourselves.

Here's what I learned through all the heartbreak of the past: In order to recognize real love, you have to know the One who created it. You have to believe that it exists because if you don't, you'll never look for it, and you'll never know how to receive it when it comes. So whether you're single, dating, or hoping for your future spouse, remember this: God's goal is not just your temporary happiness, it's your wholeness. And He's not trying to keep something good from you. He's preparing something far better than you could imagine. Don't settle for less just because it's available. Trust the timing. Trust the waiting. And most of all, trust the God who writes the very best love stories.

Your Page to Write: Where Healing Meets Action

1. Invite God Into Your Present

Today, ask God to sharpen your spiritual discernment when it comes to relationships. Instead of dwelling on past mistakes or worrying about the future, invite Him to guide how you see and respond right now.

2. Stay Present and Observant

Throughout your day, pay close attention to your reactions to people, conversations, or memories of past relationships. Notice what feelings or thoughts arise without judgment.

3. Pray for Clarity

Ask God quietly or aloud, "Lord, help me see clearly. Teach me to recognize red flags, but also to appreciate what is good, true, and from You."

4. Choose God's Spirit Over Feelings

Remind yourself not to let feelings or fears lead your decisions. Instead, invite the Holy Spirit to guide your heart and mind.

5. Practice Awareness as the First Step

Remember that discernment often starts not with a big choice, but with a daily posture of awareness. Begin today by simply being open and attentive to God's leading in the small moments.

DATING WITH DISCERNMENT

"Don't look for a partner to complete you. Look for someone who complements your completeness." [12] — *Gary Thomas*

Anyone who's ever gone grocery shopping while hungry knows it's a recipe for disaster. The smells from the deli hit you first ... the hot chicken, the creamy mac and cheese, the warm bread fresh out of the oven. Then your eyes wander to the bakery, where cookies, cakes, and every sweet imaginable call your name. You came in for a loaf of bread and leave with bags full of things you didn't plan for and probably won't even use. You spend more, get less, and often regret the whole trip.

Dating, especially in today's culture, can feel a lot like that. When we enter the dating world "hungry," emotionally starved, spiritually ungrounded, or desperate for validation, we're far more likely to walk away with more than we bargained for. We pick up patterns we never meant to carry. We attach ourselves to people who weren't sent for us. We settle for attention when what we actually need is healing. And for those who have experienced abuse, this hunger can feel especially desperate. The ache to feel seen, valued, or safe can lead us into unhealthy relationships that mirror the very trauma we're trying to escape.

So today, I want to reframe the conversation around dating, singleness, and wholeness from a place of healing, faith, and truth.

Singleness Isn't a Sickness, It's a Season

One of the greatest lies that today's culture sells us is that being single means being incomplete. But singleness is not a problem to be solved; it's a season to be stewarded. Just look at the life of Paul. He remained single and still had one of the most impactful ministries in history. His wholeness didn't come from romance, but from a radical relationship with Christ. Singleness, when seen through the lens of Scripture, is not a punishment; it's preparation.

If you're in a season of singleness, especially after coming out of a harmful or abusive relationship, don't rush the healing process just to have someone beside you. God is not late with His timing. He's being intentional. He may be using this season to rebuild you, restore your worth, and remind you that your identity is found in Him, not in who's calling, texting, or pursuing you.

Wholeness First, Then Partnership

Colossians 2:10 says, *"You are complete in Him."* When you are whole in Christ, anyone He brings into your life is just a bonus. Relationships were meant to complement us, not complete us. And for those who've known abuse, this truth is vital: A partner is not your fixer, your savior, or your escape. In fact, if someone leaves your life because you choose to put God first, let them go. If honoring your healing, boundaries, and values is "too much" for them, they're not the one.

When you know God, you begin to recognize what love

truly looks like: safe, patient, and kind, not controlling or manipulative. You don't need to guess or wonder. You just need to know God more deeply and allow His voice to be louder than any other.

I used to live in the Midwest, where the weather changed faster than your favorite playlist. One day it would snow; the next it would be sunny and 70 degrees outside. Seasons change fast. And so do our lives. Just weeks before I met my now-husband, I surrendered my desire for a relationship to God—genuinely. I told God I trusted His timing and chose to focus on His calling for me instead. Then came the shift. Out of obedience, I led worship at a camp I felt called to, and "just so happened" to meet the man I now share my life with. That said, a season of waiting isn't always short. For my husband, it had been a couple of years since he last dated before we met. But whether it's days, months, or years, God's timing is always perfect.

Abuse survivors, you don't have to look for healing in another person. Healing is already being offered in the person of Jesus. Trust His process. He won't let you miss what He has for you.

Recognizing Real Red Flags

Before I met my husband, I made a lighthearted video about silly red flags in men (think: loving black coffee, owning a Ford truck ...you get it). But here are five biblically based red flags to look for in your dating life, especially if you're healing from trauma:

1. No Long-Term Commitments

Are they stuck in short-term cycles with no evidence of

consistency? Ecclesiastes 5:5 warns, *"It is better not to vow than to make one and not fulfill it."* Patterns matter. Look for stability, not just chemistry. Consistency is a form of safety. If someone avoids defining the relationship, dodges responsibility, or always seems to have one foot out the door, you'll constantly feel unsettled. Commitment isn't just about a label. It's about showing up, again and again, even when it's not convenient. After all, God models covenant, not convenience. Don't settle for someone who only stays when it's easy.

2. Anger Issues

Watch how they treat people who have nothing to offer them. Harsh words, quick tempers, sarcastic "jokes" aren't harmless. They're seeds that can grow into emotional damage. (James 1:19-20). If someone cannot control their anger, that anger will eventually control the relationship. Anger issues may begin with yelling or sarcasm, but they can quickly turn into manipulation or emotional harm. Don't ignore those "small" flare-ups. The fruit of the Spirit includes gentleness and self-control; anything less should cause you to retreat with caution.

3. Controlling Behavior

If you feel like you're constantly being corrected, shamed, or manipulated, take a step back. Controlling behavior is rooted in fear, not love. And remember, perfect love casts out fear. (1 John 4:18). Control can be sneaky. It often starts with phrases like, "I'm just trying to protect you," or "I know what's best." But love doesn't suffocate, it sets free. If your voice starts shrinking, your opinions stop mattering, or your independence feels threatened, that's not protection. That's possession. God doesn't call you to submit to fear; He calls you to walk in freedom.

4. Patterns of Conflict

Truth be told, some people are addicted to chaos. If your peace is constantly disrupted and you're walking on eggshells, that's not love. It's trauma repeating itself. Don't confuse intensity with intimacy. High highs and low lows may feel familiar if you've been in a toxic relationship before, but that doesn't mean it's healthy. In fact, safe love sometimes feels boring to someone who's been abused because they attribute chaos to passion. Real love, however, brings clarity, not confusion. It brings peace, not panic. If every disagreement becomes a war, or if conflict is used as a way to control or punish you, that's not biblical love. It's emotional instability.

5. Misaligned Faith

You cannot build a Christ-centered future on a foundation that's divided. Don't date to convert. Wait until they are walking with Christ first, then see if God opens that door. (Matthew 12:25). A shared faith isn't just about going to church together; it's about building your lives on the same foundation. If Christ isn't the cornerstone for both of you, the house you build won't stand. You need more than spiritual interest; you need spiritual alignment. Don't compromise your convictions, hoping that someone will catch up. Wait for the one who's already walking with Jesus.

Don't Date from Your Wound, Wait on God's Will

Too many of us date from our desperation, not our destiny. We're so hungry for love that we settle for less than we deserve, sometimes, dangerously so. But hear this: You do not have to dim your light to be loved. You do not have to lower your standards to be chosen. You do not have to stay silent about your beliefs to keep someone around. And you definitely do not have to endure harm in the name of "grace." You have full permission to walk away. You have full permission to heal. And you have full permission to believe that God's best for you won't require you to betray your healing.

If God has ever removed someone from your life you thought you couldn't live without, don't panic. He's just making space. God never takes away something good without intending to replace it with something better. He didn't look at your "perfect" relationship and say, "Let Me ruin this." He said, "Let Me protect My child from what they can't yet see."

So whether you're single, dating, healing, or hoping, trust the hands of the One who holds your future. Stop shopping in your hunger. Let God fill you up, so that when love does come, it's not your lifeline, it's just the overflow.

Healing, wholeness, and holy love all start with Jesus.

Your Page to Write: Where Healing Meets Action

1. Pause and Reflect

Before stepping into a relationship, or even considering one, take a moment to ask yourself honestly: *Am I emotionally and spiritually full, or am I hungry for something only God can satisfy?*

2. Assess Your Heart

This week, pay attention to the places in your heart where you feel most "hungry" for love, validation, or connection. Write these areas down and be honest and gentle with yourself.

3. Bring Your Hunger to God

Take those thoughts and feelings to God in prayer. Ask Him to fill those empty places before anyone else does, trusting that only He can truly satisfy.

4. Journal Your Vision of Wholeness

Write about what wholeness looks like to you. What does peace feel like in your current season, whether it's singleness or healing?

5. Pray for Healing and Trust

Offer this prayer or one like it: *"Lord, heal the places in me that still ache for love in unhealthy ways. Help me trust Your timing, honor my wholeness, and never settle for less than what You've prepared for me. Fill my hunger with Your presence. Amen."*

6. Remember Your Journey

Remind yourself: you are not behind. You are being made ready. Let healing come first, and let love follow in its time.

HEALING THROUGH
HEALTHY LIMITS

"Above all else, guard your heart, for everything you do flows from it."
— *Proverbs 4:23*

I stared at the name on my phone for the tenth time. "Can we talk? I miss you," the message read. My chest tightened. I felt like I couldn't breathe. I didn't owe him anything, I knew that. We had broken up just days before. I was no longer in his grasp, but somehow, I still didn't feel free. My fingers hovered over the keyboard, paralyzed by fear and the haunting pressure to respond in a way that wouldn't provoke him. I wanted to be firm, but I also didn't want to spark his anger. I wasn't his anymore, but the control still lingered.

And then—I blocked him.

Not out of hatred or bitterness, but out of clarity. That one action felt small and terrifying, but it was the beginning of reclaiming my peace. It was the beginning of a boundary. Maybe you've felt something similar. Abuse doesn't just hurt us; it trains us to doubt our voice, question our instincts, and abandon our own safety to keep someone else calm.

Boundaries, especially after being in a controlling or manipulative relationship, can feel foreign, even wrong. But your "no" is not selfish; it's sacred. Boundaries should be set when you feel the Lord prompting you, because protecting your heart and peace is a deeply Christlike act. Setting boundaries honors both your worth and God's design for healthy love and respect.

Boundaries Are Not "Un-Christlike"

Saying no is part of reclaiming your voice. It's about rebuilding the inner trust that abuse tried to steal. God is not asking you to stay small to keep others comfortable; He's inviting you into freedom, and boundaries are part of that freedom. Jesus Himself lived with sacred boundaries. He said no. He walked away. He prioritized His spiritual well-being, and yet, He loved perfectly.

Somewhere along the way, many of us have been taught that love means being endlessly available, agreeable, or quiet. But that's not the example Christ set for us. Jesus loved without losing Himself. Yes, He laid down His life willingly, not because He had no boundaries, but because He was deeply secure in His identity and the Father's will rather than of people's demands.

Jesus regularly set boundaries in His ministry, not out of selfishness, but to seek clarity, purpose, and wisdom. If Jesus, the Son of God, didn't give everyone access to Him all the time while on earth, why do we feel guilty for needing space, rest, or protection? In Luke 5:15–16, when large crowds came to Him with urgent needs for healing, He *"withdrew to desolate places and prayed."* He didn't apologize or overextend Himself. He chose solitude because His soul needed communion with the Father more than meeting everyone's expectations. His boundary was wisdom, not rejection.

Even when others praised or followed Him enthusiastically, Jesus was discerning. John 2:23–25 tells us that although many believed in Him, *"Jesus did not entrust Himself to them … for He*

Himself knew what was in man." He did not allow everyone full access to His heart. He had an inner circle. You can love people and still protect your inner world. That's not pride, it's discernment.

When Jesus was in danger, He didn't stay to prove a point. In John 10:39, when people tried to seize Him, He escaped their grasp. He didn't stand to be mistreated or let Himself be cornered just to show strength. He removed Himself. Jesus knew walking away is sometimes the most faithful choice. Even when religious leaders tried to trap Him with manipulative questions, Jesus didn't fall into their games. He often answered with a question, redirected, or refused to respond (Luke 20:1–8). Jesus didn't feel obligated to explain Himself to those with impure motives. Likewise, you don't need to justify your boundaries to people who ignore or violate them.

Jesus loved deeply, but He didn't aim to please everyone. When many followers left in John 6:66–67, He didn't beg them to stay. Instead, He asked His disciples, *"Do you want to go away as well?"* He was grieved but didn't grasp. His love was never manipulative or desperate. He gave people the freedom to choose.

So if you've ever been told that setting boundaries is un-Christlike, that walking away, saying no, or blocking someone is selfish, look to Jesus. He wasn't driven by guilt but by clarity and compassion. His boundaries extended His love, not rejected it. If Jesus set boundaries with perfect love, you can set your own boundaries too, without fear, shame, or apology.

Lies We Believe About Saying No

When you've been in a relationship where your "no" wasn't respected or even allowed, setting boundaries doesn't just feel hard; it can feel impossible. But boundaries aren't selfish; they're sacred. They're not punishment, but protection. Not walls to keep people out but doors to let peace in. Boundaries say, "I will no longer give permission to jeopardize what God is healing in me. My heart matters. My voice matters. My healing matters."

There are many kinds of boundaries, and you have the right to all of them. Emotional boundaries say, "I'm not responsible for how others react to my feelings." Physical boundaries say, "I get to choose who touches me, how close they stand, and who enters my space." Spiritual boundaries say, "No one gets to use God to shame me into silence." Digital boundaries say, "I can unfollow, block, or delete anyone who threatens the work of Christ in me." You don't owe anyone your access or attention. You owe it to yourself and the God who loves you to choose peace in Him over people-pleasing.

Even when you know a boundary is needed, guilt, fear, and shame can creep in, especially when abuse has shaped your understanding of love. We often believe lies like:

- "If I really loved them, I'd give them another chance."
- "Maybe I'm overreacting."
- "God wouldn't want me to walk away."
- "Setting boundaries makes me bitter, cold, or unforgiving."

No. No. No. And no.

These aren't convictions; they're chains and echoes of abuse trying to silence you. You are allowed to break them. You can love someone and still walk away. You can forgive and still block. You can honor God and still say no to others. Jesus never told us to be crushed, compliant, and voiceless. He modeled bold love, not blind surrender to the people of this life. He taught us to speak truth in love (Ephesians 4:15) and guard our hearts (Proverbs 4:23). You're not selfish for protecting your peace, sinful for walking away from harm, or less loving for saying no. Boundaries protect what God is healing in you.

I shared in the introduction how I was groomed and stalked by an older man, a trusted family friend. The fear was suffocating; not just fear of what he might do, but fear of what might happen if I set a boundary. Every time I tried to say no or claim space, he responded with anger. So, I stayed small and silent, letting his comfort take priority over my safety.

But when I turned eighteen, something shifted. I realized I didn't have to live in fear. I wasn't powerless. I had a voice, and I could use it. So I did. I blocked him. I cut him off. I moved away to college and decided he would no longer have access to me, my peace, or my future. And you know what? The world didn't fall apart.

Yes, I questioned myself at times. I replayed memories, minimized the damage, and whispered excuses like, *maybe it wasn't that bad or maybe I overreacted*. Abuse trains you to gaslight yourself. But with every day of distance, I breathed more freely. I wasn't just surviving, I was healing. Setting that boundary wasn't easy. But it was holy, and it was necessary.

Here's the truth: You are allowed to protect yourself. You are allowed to walk away. You are allowed to say, "No more." Blocking isn't bitterness; it's wisdom. Creating distance isn't cruelty; it's safety. Saying no isn't betraying your faith; it's reclaiming your worth. Sometimes the most Christlike thing you can do is walk away and never look back.

Practicing Peace with Boundaries

Let's get practical. You don't need to announce your boundaries on social media or give long explanations. You don't need anyone's permission, just the Lord's prompting, courage, and practice. Boundaries don't have to be dramatic to be powerful. Start small. Practice saying no without explanation. Say, "I'm not available for that." Block or unfollow people who trigger pain or anxiety. You don't owe anyone digital access.

Write down what makes you feel safe and what doesn't. Let that list guide you. Use simple phrases in tough moments like, "I need some space right now," "That's not something I'm comfortable with," or "I appreciate your concern, but I'm not available to talk about that." You don't owe explanations to those who don't respect your voice. Kindness and firmness can coexist.

You will feel guilty, and that's normal. You may be called selfish, and that's expected. You may lose relationships, and that's heartbreaking, but freeing. People who thrived on your silence won't like your strength, and those who depended on your compliance won't understand your confidence. But you don't answer to them. You answer to a God who is tender with your heart and serious about your freedom. That pushback stings, but it doesn't mean you're wrong.

Not everyone will understand your boundaries, and they don't have to. God does. If you're afraid, remember that you're not the person who couldn't say no anymore. You're becoming the woman who knows her worth and defends it, not with rage, but with grace and wisdom.

Boundaries aren't bitterness or fear-based self-protection. They're participation in your healing. They say to God, "I trust You more than my fear. I trust You enough to leave the door closed when You say no, and to walk away from what You never asked me to carry." Boundaries help rebuild trust with yourself, love others from health rather than obligation, and hear the Holy Spirit's voice louder than shame.

You're not being dramatic or unkind when you set boundaries. You're being faithful—faithful to healing, faithful to God's voice, and faithful to the woman He's shaping you into. Your healing is holy. Protect it with everything you've got.

Your Page to Write: Where Healing Meets Action

1. Define Your Boundary

Take some time this week to clearly identify one boundary that will protect your peace and support your healing. Write it down plainly, without feeling the need to justify or apologize for it.

2. Practice Your Boundary in a Small Way

Choose one simple way to put that boundary into action. It might be saying "no" without explaining yourself, blocking someone who continues to cause harm, or setting a clear limit on your time or energy.

3. Remember Why Boundaries Matter

Know this: your "no" is not selfish. Boundaries are biblical and essential for healing. You're not shutting others out from fear, but stepping into faith by protecting the work God is doing in you.

4. Pray for Strength and Wisdom

If it helps, pray something like this: *"Lord, help me guard what You are healing in me. Give me courage to say no, wisdom to know when to walk away, and peace to stand firm in love. Amen."*

5. Stand Firm in Love

Trust that setting healthy boundaries is part of your journey toward wholeness. Each small step of protection is an act of faith in God's healing power.

COMMUNICATING YOUR
PAST TO YOUR PRESENT

"To be loved but not known is comforting but superficial. To be known and not loved is our greatest fear. But to be fully known and truly loved ... is a lot like being loved by God."[13] — *Tim Keller*

There are certain moments in life when time seems to stand still. For me, one of those moments came the night I handed my now-husband a piece of my story I had never shared in full. Up until then, I had only hinted at the ache I carried. I'd made small comments, careful disclosures. "I've been through some things," I'd say. "That relationship really hurt me." He never pressed. He never pried. But one night, in a quiet conversation that had wandered into deeper waters, he looked at me with steady eyes and said, "Whenever you're ready, I want to know your story. All of it."

My heart thudded in my chest. I had waited so long to be seen, yet the idea of being fully known was terrifying. Speaking the words out loud felt impossible. It was too messy and too raw. But I had written them. My therapist had encouraged me to put it all on paper a while ago, and I had. Every memory. Every scar. Every moment I thought had broken me beyond repair. So instead of speaking, I handed him my journal.

It was the closest thing to my soul I could offer. The pages were stained with grief, shame, fear, survival, and slow healing. I held my breath as he opened it, bracing myself for distance, judgment, discomfort, or silence I'd known too well from others.

But that's not what he gave me.

He read each page slowly and carefully, like my pain was sacred ground. Not once did he look away. When he finally closed the journal, his eyes met mine. They were full of compassion, but there was something even deeper: honor. And then he said something I'll never forget. "Can I keep it? Not to hold onto your pain, but to protect it. To remind me of what you've walked through, and what I promise to walk with you from now on."

Something inside me made a continental shift, because in that moment, I wasn't just heard. I was held.

That night marked the beginning of a new kind of love, where my trauma wasn't a burden to be tolerated but a part of me to be cherished. He didn't rescue me. He didn't fix me. He simply stayed and loved me regardless. And for someone whose story had been marked by abandonment and the wrong definition of love, that kind of presence was its own kind of healing.

That night changed everything. Not just in our relationship, but in how I viewed my own story. For the first time, I saw that my past didn't make me "too much." It didn't scare him away. Instead, it drew him closer. But that moment didn't come out of nowhere. It took time. Healing. Waiting. Counseling. Praying. And courage that I didn't think I had.

I know how overwhelming it can feel to open up about your trauma, especially when your past has taught you that vulnerability isn't safe. Maybe you've tried before and been met with silence, shame, or even rejection. Maybe you've kept your story locked away so long it feels like a foreign language to speak out loud. If that's you, I see you. I've been you.

In the rest of this chapter, I want to walk with you through the process of how to share your story, not all at once, not perfectly, but bravely. We'll talk about how to know when you're ready, how to recognize safe people, and how to communicate your pain in a way that invites connection without compromising your healing. This isn't a formula. It's a journey. But it starts with one small, sacred decision that you deserve to be known. Not in a way that's just the shiny, healed parts, but the wounded ones too. And there are people, maybe just one person, who will hold your story the way mine was held: with gentleness, respect, and love. Let's talk about how to get there.

How to Know When You're Ready to Share Your Story

There is no perfect moment to share your trauma. There's no blinking sign or clear green light that tells you now's the time. Sometimes, readiness is quietly unfolding. Sometimes it's a whisper in your spirit that says, *You're safe now.* But how can you tell if you're truly ready?

For me, the first sign came when I had finally faced the story for myself. Before I could ever hand it to someone else, I had to sit with it in the privacy of my own heart. I had to write it out, cry through it, pray over it, and begin to understand how deeply it had shaped me. If you haven't yet faced your story in a way that allows you to name what happened and feel the weight of it, then sharing it out loud may feel more wounding than healing. Telling someone else isn't the first step in recovery; it's a continuation of the healing you've already begun.

I also knew I was ready because something inside me shifted from just wanting to be heard to genuinely wanting to be known. I wasn't looking for someone to rescue or fix me anymore. I didn't need a solution. I needed a witness, someone to hold space for my pain without trying to edit it. If that desire is stirring in you, not just for someone to listen, but to really see you, that's a tender sign of readiness.

Another important piece is recognizing what parts of your story you actually want to share. You don't owe anyone every detail. Being ready doesn't mean you hand someone the whole book. It might mean you share just a page, or even a sentence. For example, the story I shared with my husband included far more detail than the story I would share in front of my church congregation. You get to choose your boundaries. Readiness means you've started to discern which parts of your past matter most in this season, and you're able to say, "This part is still mine for now."

Of course, readiness also depends on who you're sharing with. Even if you feel emotionally prepared, the person hearing your story matters deeply. Are they safe? Do they listen well? Have they earned the right to hold something so sacred? A safe person won't rush you, fix you, or twist your story. They will receive it with gentleness, grace, and deep respect. I'll talk more about how to recognize a safe person in the next section, but for now, simply ask yourself, *Does this person create peace in me, or pressure?* That answer matters.

And finally, I believe you're ready when your story begins to feel like a bridge instead of a wall. You may still feel nervous or afraid (I certainly did), but if there's even the smallest flicker of hope ... hope that someone might meet you in your pain and stay ... then you're already halfway there. You don't need to be perfectly healed. You don't need to have all the right words. You just need a willingness to say, "This is part of me, and I want to share it with you." That willingness, fragile as it feels, is holy. It is brave. It is enough.

Sharing Your Story: How to Say It and What You Don't Have to Say

There's no single right way to tell your story. Some people speak their truth in a single conversation. Others need time, journaling, art, or prayer before they ever say it out loud. What matters most isn't *how* you communicate your trauma, but that you feel safe and supported while doing it. The method should match your heart, not someone else's expectations.

For me, writing was my safest beginning. I couldn't speak my pain … not yet. But I could write it. My journal became a space where I could tell the truth without interruption, without fear of judgment, and without anyone staring back. When I finally gave that journal to the man who would become my husband, I was handing him the most fragile part of my story in the way that felt least threatening to me. You might find that works for you, too. It may feel more natural to write a letter, a poem, or a few paragraphs rather than having a face-to-face talk.

Others may feel ready to speak their story out loud, but even then, it's okay to prepare. You can rehearse with a counselor, a trusted friend, or even out loud to yourself. You can write notes or keep phrases nearby that help you stay centered. And if the words get stuck, that doesn't mean you've failed; it just means your heart is tender. Let grace meet you there.

Some people express their story through art, music, movement, or metaphors. You don't have to describe every event in detail, and it's probably best that you don't. Sometimes, the most powerful communication happens through symbols. For example, saying, "This shaped me" without retelling every scene, or something as simple as, "I experienced some things in my past that still impact me today. I'm still healing, but I want to invite you into that process." That's real, and that's enough.

And here's something important to remember: You don't owe anyone the full version. You do not have to relive every detail. You don't have to explain every reaction. You don't have to be fully healed to start talking about what hurt you. In fact, sometimes healing begins because you let someone into the room with you. What you share is your choice. Your pace. Your right. That puts the power in your hands. Sometimes we fear that if we don't say everything, we're being dishonest. But honesty doesn't mean exposure; it means authenticity. And authenticity can sound like, "There's more to this part of my life, but I'm not ready to talk about it yet." That's a boundary. And that's brave.

So whether you share your story in paragraphs or fragments, with eye contact or on paper, let it be an act of freedom and power, not pressure. Let it be slow if it needs to be. Let it be imperfect. Let it be yours.

What Happens After: When You're Met with Love or When You're Not

After you share your story, there's that daunting moment when time seems to stand still. When the air seems to hold its breath. You've opened your heart, maybe for the first time. You've let someone see behind the curtain, and now you wait, wondering: *Will they stay? Will they still want me? Will they handle this with care?*

Sometimes, that moment becomes one of the most healing experiences of your life. That's what happened to me. When I handed over my journal, I expected hesitation, confusion, questions, distance, and shame. Instead, I was met with steady compassion. My story wasn't too much. It was honored. Held. Cherished. When my husband asked to keep the journal, not out of obligation but as a symbol of his promise to protect what was vulnerable in me, I realized something. I wasn't alone in my healing anymore.

Maybe you'll have that moment too. Maybe the person you choose will respond with gentleness, with awe at your courage, and with the kind of love that whispers, *You're still safe. You're still loved. I'm not going anywhere.* If that happens, let yourself receive it. Let the kindness wash over the places where pain once ruled. Let that moment be a turning point, not because someone saved you, but because someone stayed.

But what if they don't? What if you share your story and it's met with discomfort, silence, judgment, or worse, rejection? First, let me say this as clearly as I can: Their reaction is not a reflection of your worth. Someone's inability to handle your story does not mean your story shouldn't have been told. It doesn't mean you were wrong to speak. It doesn't mean your pain was too much. Sometimes, people lack the maturity, empathy, or experience to know how to respond to vulnerability. That's not your fault. That's not your shame to carry. And it does not undo your progress. In fact, naming your truth, even when it's not received well, is still a victory. It's still a step forward.

And here's something to consider: A difficult reaction doesn't always mean that person isn't meant to be in your life. It might simply mean they still have work to do. Healing often requires both people to grow. What matters is whether they're willing to do that work to meet you in a place of safety and honesty. If they shut down or refuse, that's revealing too. But if they lean in with humility and a desire to learn, that's worth paying attention to.

Still, I won't sugarcoat it: Rejection can sting deeply. For survivors of trauma, it can send us spiraling back into old wounds, making us feel like the same abandonment or dismissal is happening all over again. If you find yourself in that space, pause and breathe. Remind yourself of what's true: One person's reaction does not rewrite your identity or the progress you've made. Step outside of the story in your head and anchor yourself in God's voice instead. You are loved. You are seen. You are not back to the beginning. You are still moving forward in power, strength, and beauty.

We also have to acknowledge the culture we live in. Society isn't always equipped for deep, raw conversations about trauma. That's why so many of us default to "I'm good" when someone asks how we are. And that's okay. There is room for both experiences: the space where you protect your heart with small talk, and the space where you open your soul with trusted people who can hold it. Both are valid. Both are part of living in a world that doesn't always know what to do with pain.

So if someone doesn't respond the way you hoped, don't let it silence you. You are not too much. Your story still matters. And there are safe, God-given people who will listen, not perfectly, but faithfully. Don't give up on being known.

The truth is, telling your story will never be easy, but it will always be holy. Every time you choose truth over silence, healing over hiding, and connection over fear, you reclaim something sacred that trauma tried to steal: your voice. You are not defined by what happened to you. You are defined by the courage it takes to rise, to speak, and to love again anyway. Sharing your story isn't just about being understood; it's about letting someone step into the most fragile part of your heart and stay. Whether you speak it out loud, write it on a page, or whisper it through tears, your story is worth telling, and you are worthy of being known, fully and without fear.

Your Page to Write: Where Healing Meets Action

1. Assess Your Readiness

Begin by gently checking in with yourself. Do you feel ready to share your story? Give yourself full permission to take all the time and space you need to process your experiences privately through writing, prayer, or quiet reflection.

2. Choose a Safe Person

When you feel ready, identify someone you trust who will listen without judgment, respect your boundaries, and honor your vulnerability.

3. Decide What and How to Share

Decide how much you want to share and in what way. It's okay to start small, maybe with just a few sentences, or to share in writing instead of speaking. Move at the pace that feels right for you.

4. Prepare for Varied Responses

Be ready for a range of reactions. Remember, how others respond doesn't define your worth or the truth of your story. Your experience and your healing are valid, no matter what.

5. Reclaim Your Voice and Invite Healing

This step is about reclaiming your voice and opening the door to authentic connection on your terms. Trust God's guidance as you take this brave step forward.

TURN THE PAGE

"Therefore, if anyone is in Christ, the new creation has come: The old has gone, the new is here!" — 2 Corinthians 5:17

Pain has a way of becoming part of our identity, if we're not careful. It starts quietly through heartbreak, betrayal, or deep disappointment. Before we know it, the wounds we carry become the lens we see everything through. We start to define ourselves by what we've been through, instead of by who God says we are. The scars begin to speak louder than Scripture. And eventually, without meaning to, we start living not from a place of purpose but from a place of pain.

In student ministry, I see this all the time. Teenagers sit across from me with tears in their eyes, sharing stories of neglect, bullying, insecurity, abandonment, and abuse. These are real wounds. Real trauma. As a worship leader and small group leader, I've had the privilege of walking alongside these students, listening with an open heart, and offering a safe space for them to share what has often been hidden for years. I've led discussions, prayed over hearts, and tried to create moments in worship where they could encounter God's presence and feel seen. I do my best to honor every story, gently pointing them toward the truth that their identity is found in Christ, not in the pain they've endured. And yet, even with prayer and guidance, I've noticed a pattern: many still feel more comfortable calling themselves victims than embracing the reality that they are beloved children of God.

We live in a culture that often glorifies trauma. It's trendy to be broken, relatable to be bitter. Pain can become currency for attention. As a result, healing becomes too costly because it asks us to release the identity we've grown attached to. But friends, let me say this plainly: God never called you to live as a prisoner of your past. He came to set you free. And freedom isn't found in staying in the dark. Freedom is found when you turn toward the Light.

The Invitation to Remember Differently

In Exodus 12, God tells the Israelites to commemorate the Passover. This came after the death of Egypt's firstborns—a tragic, terrifying night. Yet God tells His people to celebrate it. Why? Because it marked their deliverance. It marked the night God pulled them out of slavery and into freedom. God didn't ask them to relive the years they spent in bondage and pain. He asked them to remember His faithfulness.

What would happen if we started doing that? What if we turned our trauma anniversaries into deliverance anniversaries? What if we stopped remembering just the hurt and started celebrating the healing? What if we stopped telling stories about how we were broken and started sharing testimonies about how we were restored?

From Brokenness to Brightness

You've probably seen how a glowstick works. It doesn't light up until it's been bent and cracked. Something has to give before it shines. And in a way, healing is like that too. The places in your story that feel broken or bent beyond repair might be the very places where God's light pours through the most. The pain may be part of your past, but it doesn't get to define your future. And it doesn't get to be the brightest thing about you.

God's healing isn't just about helping you feel better. It's about helping you live free, whole, and awake to purpose again. He doesn't just restore your heart; He redeems your story. Because the truth is, you weren't just rescued *from* something dark. You were rescued *for* something good.

After trauma, it's easy to feel like you're just surviving. Like you've lost your light and are overcome by the dark. But the Lord made you on purpose and for a purpose. And that purpose didn't vanish with your trauma. The Lord is still using you for good and still calling you to something better.

God has personal and unique plans for each of us. But He's also given us a shared invitation to be salt and light in a world that desperately needs both. In Matthew 5, Jesus says we are the salt of the earth and the light of the world. Not because we're polished or put together, but because we reflect the One who is.

Jesus told us to let our light shine before others, not so people would admire us, but so they would see Him in us. It's not about stepping into the spotlight or trying to appear perfect. We aren't the source of the light; we're simply the reflection. On our own, we can't illuminate anything. But when we turn our hearts toward Jesus, the true Light of the world, His light begins to shine through us.

Think of the moon. It doesn't glow because of anything within itself. It's just a quiet, lifeless rock until it turns toward the sun. Then it lights up the night. That's what we do when we stay close to Jesus. We reflect His light, even when we feel worn out, cracked open, or unqualified.

Jesus also called us the salt of the earth, and that carries just as much weight. Salt preserves. In ancient times, it kept meat from spoiling. In a world that's slowly decaying under the weight of sin, God has placed us here to help preserve what is good and true. We hold onto His Word, we carry the hope of the Gospel, and we live in a way that resists the rot.

Salt also adds flavor. In the same way, your life, transformed by Jesus, brings something sacred into the ordinary. It makes people curious. It makes them thirsty for something more. When you live like you've been healed and redeemed, people begin to ask questions. They notice. They wonder.

But here's the thing: Salt only works if it's used. And light only matters if it's seen. If we blend in so much with the world that no one can tell the difference, we're missing the mission. Jesus didn't save us so we could stay hidden. He saved us to stand out, not with noise or pride, but with love, humility, and truth.

Being salt and light isn't about having it all together. It's about staying close to the Source. It's about letting your story point to the One who's still writing it. You don't have to be perfect to make an impact. You just have to be willing to shine.

So what does that mean for your healing? It means you don't have to wait until you're completely "better" to live like you're loved and called. You don't have to cover up the cracks or the scars. You just have to stay turned toward the Light. The same

God who hung the stars in the sky is the One who gives your light a reason to shine.

So let it shine. Not in perfection, but in reflection.

Moving from Victim to Victor

There comes a point in every healing journey where we have to make a choice: *Will I keep replaying what they did to me, or will I choose to focus on what Christ did for me?* Because here's the truth: if what people did *to* you is louder in your life than what Jesus did *for* you, you'll always stay stuck. But if Christ becomes the loudest voice in your story, you'll start to live in victory and shine brighter than ever.

In John 5, Jesus meets a man who had been sick for thirty-eight years. And He asks a question that, at first glance, seems ridiculous: *"Do you want to be healed?"* Of course, he did, right? But maybe Jesus asked that because He knew something we often ignore: Some people don't want to be healed, because healing requires change. Healing requires facing the truth. Healing requires letting go of the attention, the identity, and the story we've wrapped ourselves in.

I've been that person. After breaking up with someone who had manipulated and abused me, I found myself in a spiral of anxiety and depression. I thought my story would end there. I wore heartbreak like a label. I believed I was damaged goods. But God, in His mercy, stepped in and whispered to my soul: *Enough.* Enough living like a victim. Enough carrying the chains that Christ already broke. Enough letting someone else's sin write the end of my story. I had to choose to believe God had more for me than the ashes I was sitting in. I had to turn the page. And you can too.

So do it. You don't have to be known by your pain. You don't have to keep rehearsing the worst parts of your story. You don't have to wait for someone else to fix what only God can heal. He's already written the ending, and it's one of hope, of redemption, and victory. But you have to make the choice to keep moving forward. Your pain is real, but so is your healing. Your trauma is valid, but so is your freedom. Your past may have shaped you, but it does not define you. You are not just what you've been through. You are what Christ died to redeem.

Now I ask you the same question Jesus asked: Do you want to be healed? If the answer is yes, then it's time.

Take a deep breath. Lift your eyes. And turn the page.

Your Page to Write: Where Healing Meets Action

1. Make the Choice to Begin

Today, decide with intention to stop living in your pain and start living in God's healing. This is a courageous first step, one that honors your journey and your hope.

2. Let God's Light Shine Through Your Brokenness

Invite God's healing presence to fill your wounds and transform your scars into stories of hope. Your brokenness is not your identity. It's the place where His light shines brightest.

3. Anchor Yourself in the Truth of Freedom

Remind yourself daily: Your past does not define you. Freedom does. When old pain tries to resurface, return to this truth with prayer, Scripture, or the support of trusted people who walk with you.

4. Walk Forward With Courage and Grace

Healing is a process, not a destination. Take each step with patience and trust that God is shaping a beautiful, new story —your story.

5. Turn the Page

Now, with courage and grace, turn the page. Close the chapter of pain and open the next, filled with God's healing, hope, and promise. Your past no longer holds you, freedom does. It's time to walk forward, healed, whole, and deeply loved.

END NOTES

1. Bell Hooks, All About Love: New Visions (New York: William Morrow Paperbacks, 2018).
2. Legal Information Institute, "Abuse," Cornell Law School, accessed August 15, 2025, https://www.law.cornell.edu/wex/abuse.
3. The National Domestic Violence Hotline, "Types of Abuse," accessed August 15, 2025, https://www.thehotline.org/resources/types-of-abuse/.
4. Joni Eareckson Tada, "Show Me How to Live," transcript, Joni and Friends Radio, March 27, 2024, https://joniandfriendsradio.simplecast.com/episodes/show-me-how-to-live/transcript.
5. Rick Warren, The Purpose Driven Life: What on Earth Am I Here For? (Grand Rapids, MI: Zondervan, 2002).
6. C. S. Lewis, Mere Christianity (New York: HarperOne, 2001).
7. Steven Furtick, Crash the Chatterbox: Hearing God's Voice Above All Others (Colorado Springs, CO: Multnomah Books, 2014).
8. Lysa TerKeurst, Forgiving What You Can't Forget: Discover How to Move On, Make Peace with Painful Memories, and Create a Life That's Beautiful Again (Nashville, TN: Thomas Nelson, 2020).
9. World Health Organization, "Post-Traumatic Stress Disorder," WHO Fact Sheet, May 27, 2024, https://www.who.int/news-room/fact-sheets/detail/post-traumatic-stress-disorder.
10. Oswald Chambers, My Utmost for His Highest (Grand Rapids, MI: Discovery House, 1935).
11. Bob Goff, Love Does: Discover a Secretly Incredible Life in an Ordinary World (Nashville, TN: Thomas Nelson, 2012).
12. Gary Thomas, The Sacred Search: What If It's Not About Who You Marry, But Why? (Grand Rapids, MI: Zondervan, 2013).
13. Timothy Keller, The Meaning of Marriage: Facing the Complexities of Commitment with the Wisdom of God (New York: Dutton, 2011).

Resources for Women Healing from Abuse

National Domestic Violence Hotline
1-800-799-SAFE (7233)
https://thehotline.org

Focus on the Family – Counseling Services
1-855-771-HELP (4357)
https://www.focusonthefamily.com/get-help/

Celebrate Recovery
Christ-centered recovery groups
https://www.celebraterecovery.com/

Christian Women's Job Corps
Empowering women through Christ-centered classes and mentoring
https://wmu.com/cwjc/

RAINN (Rape, Abuse & Incest National Network)
Confidential support 24/7
https://www.rainn.org/

A21
Global anti-human trafficking organization
https://www.a21.org/

Church-Based Counseling
Contact your local church or pastor for biblically sound counseling resources.

CONNECT WITH THE AUTHOR

Thank you so much for reading *Turn the Page.* I'm truly honored to walk alongside you on your journey toward healing, freedom, and identity in Christ. It means the world to me that these words have found their way into your hands and heart.

To receive monthly encouragement, devotionals, and biblical resources, visit **Stay Rooted Ministries** at www.stayrootedministries.com. There you'll find blog posts, spiritual growth tools, and ways to connect with a community rooted in faith.

You can also listen to my original worship music on Spotify and other streaming platforms. Just search for "**Jordyn St. John**" to discover songs inspired by my own journey of faith and healing.

I'm available for speaking engagements, worship leading, songwriting, or podcast guest appearances. If you would like to invite me to your event or ministry, please visit the **Services** page on Stay Rooted Ministries to get in touch or email connect@stayrootedministries.com.

If *Turn the Page* has spoken to your soul, encouraged your healing, or sparked hope in your heart, please reach out. Your story matters deeply to me because healing is not meant to be walked alone. Together, we are stronger. Together, we can embrace the freedom and identity God has for us.

Thank you for trusting me with this part of your journey. May you always know you are deeply loved, fully valued, and never alone.

Let's keep turning the page—one step, one prayer, and one story at a time.

YOUR PAGE TO WRITE

YOUR PAGE TO WRITE

YOUR PAGE TO WRITE

YOUR PAGE TO WRITE

YOUR PAGE TO WRITE

YOUR PAGE TO WRITE

YOUR PAGE TO WRITE

YOUR PAGE TO WRITE

YOUR PAGE TO WRITE

YOUR PAGE TO WRITE